From Here to Free Trade

T0364184

From Here to Free Trade
Essays in Post–Uruguay Round Trade Strategy

Ernest H. Preeg

Center for Strategic and International Studies
Washington

The University of Chicago Press
Chicago and London

ERNEST H. PREEG holds the William M. Scholl Chair in International Business at the Center for Strategic and International Studies in Washington, D.C. He was a U.S. trade negotiator in the GATT Kennedy Round in the 1960s and in the Uruguay Round in the 1980s. His previous books include *Traders and Diplomats* (1970), *Economic Blocs and U.S. Foreign Policy* (1974), *The American Challenge in World Trade* (1989), and *Traders in a Brave New World* (1995).

The University of Chicago Press, Chicago 60637
The University of Chicago Press, Ltd., London
©1998 by The University of Chicago
All rights reserved. Published in 1998
Printed in the United States of America
07 06 05 04 03 02 01 00 99 98   1 2 3 4 5
ISBN: 0-226-67961-6   (cloth)
ISBN: 0-226-67962-4   (paper)

Library of Congress Cataloging-in-Publication Data

Preeg, Ernest H.
    From here to free trade : essays in post–Uruguay round trade strategy / Ernest H. Preeg.
        p.   cm.
    "Published in cooperation with the Center for Strategic & International Studies."
    Includes bibliographical references and index.
    ISBN 0-226-67961-6 (cloth : alk. paper). — ISBN 0-226-67962-4 (paper : alk. paper)
    1. Free trade—United States.   2. United States—Commercial policy.   3. United States—Foreign economic relations.   4. Uruguay Round (1987–1994)   5. International trade.   I. Title.
HF1756.P68   1998
382'.71'0973—dc21   97-35616
                                                                        CIP

Contents

Preface

This collection of essays, produced during 1996–97, is to a large extent a follow-on volume to my *Traders in a Brave New World: The Uruguay Round and the Future of the International Trading System*, also published by the University of Chicago Press in late 1995. The earlier work is an analytic history of the Uruguay Round period, from the first U.S. call to action in 1981 through the official opening of the World Trade Organization (WTO) in 1995. This time of transformation for trade and the trading system set the stage for what will come next in international economic relationships. These new circumstances will require that the United States formulate a comprehensive trade strategy, and the essays presented here address the major issues that will determine what this strategy should be.

The years 1995–97 were a time of hiatus and indecision for trade policy. The United States, the traditional leader in trade policy formulation, was preoccupied with domestic politics leading up to the November 1996 presidential elections, wherein further trade liberalizing initiatives were considered bad politics by both major political parties. The general assumption was that, beginning in 1997, renewed U.S. leadership would be forthcoming to formulate a post–Uruguay Round trade strategy, based in part on various elements of policy already in train and in part on new initiatives, all fitting together in an overall plan of action, but such formulation has been slow to materialize. Meanwhile, there has been considerable trade policy strategizing outside of governments—among experts, private sector leaders, and ex-officio government officials—from which most of these essays derive.

The opening essay, "Economic Globalization and the U.S. National Interest: A Net Assessment," appears here for the first time, although it also is being used as a conceptual underpinning for a new CSIS project on the "New Global Economy." It describes the current "wave" of globalization, finds it to be distinct from and more far-reaching in its impact than earlier periods of deepening economic relationships, and assesses U.S. interests in terms of economic growth and productivity, adjustments to the national economy, and national sovereignty/security. The findings indicate that the gains in economic growth and productivity tend to be understated, the adjustment costs overstated, and that the wrong questions are being asked about the relationship between economic globalization and national sovereignty/security. The overall net assessment supports a continued U.S. liberal trade policy, although it is a contingent assessment that will become more so over the longer term.

The second essay, "The Post–Uruguay Round Free Trade Debate," is a revised version of an article published in the winter 1996 edition of *The Washington Quarterly*. It summarizes the post–Uruguay Round trade policy setting, particularly with regard to recent moves toward free trade at both the multilateral and regional levels, which constitutes a new and sharply different set of circumstances for formulating trade strategy in the period ahead. The essay also highlights the growing leadership role of the private sector, in the United States and other countries, in stimulating liberal trade policy initiatives.

The ensuing three essays deal with the principal regional economic relationships of the United States—Europe, the Americas, and East Asia. "Free Trade Across the Atlantic" also appeared first in *The Washington Quarterly*, in spring 1996, and is updated and expanded substantially in the presentation here. The case is made for a serious, sympathetic examination of a Transatlantic Free Trade Agreement (TAFTA), which has not yet been done despite Secretary of State Warren Christopher's commitment in June 1995 to do so. The three principal dimensions of a TAFTA are examined: the direct trade effects, the impact on the evolution of the world trading system, and the relationship to U.S. foreign policy objectives.

"Regulatory Regimes in World Trade: The Case of NAFTA and the FTAA" was first presented at a conference organized by the Research Institute for International Affairs in Munich in July 1996, as part of a volume of papers on regulatory policies and world trade, published by the Institute in 1997. Within the context of the decision by Western Hemisphere leaders to conclude a regional free trade agreement by 2005, the essay analyzes the terms of reference and preparatory work underway in nine established working groups dealing with a wide range of trade-related policies with heavy regulatory content—including

investment and competition policies, industrial and phytosanitary standards, public procurement, intellectual property rights,
trade in services, and rules of origin—both with respect to their
potential impact on trade and their compatibility with corresponding regulatory regimes being developed within the WTO,
the European Union, and across the Pacific. A central conclusion is that institution-building for such regulatory policies in
Western Hemisphere developing countries should be a major
positive result from a Free Trade Agreement of the Americas
(FTAA), which in almost all cases would reinforce commitments already undertaken within the WTO. The presentation
also demonstrates that an FTAA, if successfully negotiated,
would indeed be comprehensive in scope, or relatively "deep"
integration in current trade policy parlance.

"APEC and the Interregional Triad" was originally written
for a conference on Europe and Asia-Pacific Economic Cooperation (APEC) in Brussels in October 1996, organized by the
European Institute for Asian Studies. The version presented
here updates and expands the assessment of APEC, particularly
with respect to the commitment to achieve regional free trade
by 2010/2020, which faces faltering credibility. The broader context of the essay, however, relates APEC, as the intergovernmental economic policy bridge between North America and East
Asia, to two more recent and still ill-defined interregional initiatives, the New Transatlantic Agenda and Asia-Europe Meeting
(ASEM), and assesses possible interactions among the three
dimensions of this "interregional triad."

Finally, "From Here to Free Trade: The Quest for a Multilat-
eral/Regional Synthesis," pulls together elements of all of the
preceding essays in a self-contained statement that addresses the
overarching theme of the volume, as expressed in the subtitle,
namely the need to integrate the now largely separate multilateral and regional tracks of the world trading system. Three
alternative scenarios are presented for such integration, the first
to continue the current two separate track course, leaving a
formal synthesis for later, the second a WTO free trade "Grand
Bargain," and the third an extension and integration of regional
free trade groupings, featuring a TAFTA as a key catalytic step.
The third scenario of progressive integration among regional
groupings is judged preferable, but it is a complex scenario in
need of more thorough analysis. This essay also forms part of a
broader project on U.S. trade strategy organized by Geza
Feketekuty, director of the Center for Trade and Commercial

Diplomacy at the Monterey Institute of International Studies, and cosponsored by the Council of Foreign Relations and CSIS. The resulting collection of papers was published in 1997.

The quest for such a multilateral/regional synthesis remains elusive, as illustrated throughout these essays, and yet its specification is central to the formulation of a comprehensive, coherent U.S. trade policy for the period ahead. It is also a pressing concern as illustrated by two major events in 1998, one regional and the other multilateral in character. The regional event is the summit meeting in Santiago, Chile, in April, to launch negotiations for free trade and investment among the thirty-four market-oriented democracies in the Western Hemisphere. The multilateral event is the WTO ministerial meeting in Geneva in May to commemorate the fiftieth anniversary of the predecessor GATT organization and to begin discussion of what comes next for trade liberalization on a multilateral basis. As explained in what follows, these two events establish the basic moorings for U.S. trade policy development over the next several years.

Another recurring, related theme during 1995–97 was the striking irony in U.S. trade strategy whereby regional free trade objectives were more comprehensive and far-reaching than the multilateral WTO agenda. The United States is committed to free trade and investment across the Pacific by 2010, to a similar agreement in the Americas by 2005, and to a sweeping yet still largely undefined New Transatlantic Marketplace with Europe. In contrast, the United States uncharacteristically resisted any grand design or even "new round" of multilateral negotiations in the WTO, preferring limited item-by-item negotiations, mostly old business loose ends from the Uruguay Round agreement. A broader conceptual and operational focus on multilateral objectives is needed and is belatedly being addressed, but this can only be done in conjunction with the already established regional free trade objectives.

A quarter century ago I wrote a book entitled *Economic Blocs and U.S. Foreign Policy,* in which I summarized the prospect for the trading system in the following terms: "There is a fundamental link between the evolution of a tripolar economic relationship among the advanced industrialized countries and the structure of the world economic system. The phenomenon of economic tripolarization may, in fact, prove to be the crucial empirical factor over the foreseeable future for deriving the most sensible ordering of the international economy, be it in terms of multilateral rules, of more limited economic-bloc arrangements, or—as is most likely—of some combination of the two" (National Planning Association, 1974, p. 9). In retrospect, this statement has held up rather well, but with the distinction that what was then a long-term projection has now become an immediate policy challenge, how to formulate "some combination of the two," or in other words the quest for a multilateral/regional synthesis.

This collection of essays provides an assessment of these broad issues of trade strategy, with a focus on their interrelationships, but it is far from the final word on the subject. The world economy is going through a period of fundamental change and evolution in international economic relationships that will have far-reaching impact on daily life in America as well as on U.S. interests elsewhere in the world. In this context, the intent here is in large part to stimulate thought, provoke debate, and understand better where we are going as a nation in the inevitable "new global economy." The net assessment drawn here is positive and optimistic as to U.S. interests in a more and more open world economy, but as noted above, it is a contingent assessment, requiring sustained and, at times, bold policy formulation and implementation. If nothing else, this volume should define such contingencies more clearly as we go from here to free trade.

I am deeply grateful to the many readers, too numerous to list, who provided comments on these essays at various stages of formulation. I also wish to express special thanks to my research assistant, René Brun, for indefatigable work in gathering materials and analyzing data, and to my administrative assistant, Andrea Williams, for dedicated organizational and secretarial support throughout.

1

Economic Globalization and the U.S. National Interest: A Net Assessment

Economic globalization is the catchphrase for where the world is heading, but the term is ill-defined and poorly understood.[1] As a consequence, opinion varies widely as to what economic globalization means for the course of world events and for U.S. interests in particular. Some believe it is having a substantial net positive effect on U.S. interests, others a substantial net negative effect, and still others little significant effect at all.

One reason for this muddled state of mind is the deluge of episodic reports which, while making for good debating points, can be selectively misleading.[2] A more fundamental reason is the inherent complexity of the current economic globalization process and the limited amount of information available about some of its key workings. Systematic analysis tends to be either of the forest or trees variety: sweeping commentary about globalization in futuristic terms which does not lend itself to specific conclusions, or intensive examination of particular segments of the globalization process whose findings cannot be extrapolated to a broader assessment.

The presentation here falls somewhere between these two extremes, producing both relatively broad-based and specific results. The major elements of the economic globalization process are identified and described in quantitative and qualitative terms to the limited extent feasible. The major categories of impact on U.S. interests are then examined, leading to an overall net assessment. There are important analytic and empirical gaps, and pointing them up as priorities for further investigation is a useful result in itself. Even on the limited basis of this presentation, however, some fairly clear conclusions can be drawn as to U.S. interests in the economic globalization process and the consequent appropriate policy responses, particularly for trade and trade-related policies.

This essay is divided into six sections. The first describes the distinctive characteristics of the current "wave" of economic globalization, and concludes that it is both very different and far more important than past waves. The following section adds quantitative and qualitative dimensions to this conclusion in terms of trade, foreign direct investment (FDI), nonequity affiliations, and other cross-border economic activities. The ensuing three sections address the principal categories of impact on U.S. national interests, namely, productivity and economic growth, the national economic adjustment process, and national sovereignty/security. The findings are that the positive productivity/economic growth effects tend to be understated, that the costs of adjustment overstated, and that the wrong questions are being asked about national sovereignty/security. The final section, drawing on all of the foregoing, presents a broadly positive net assessment of the impact of economic globalization on U.S. interests, and thus supports, inter alia, a continued liberal trade policy, but with important contingencies that become more important over time.

Distinguishing Characteristics

Economic globalization can be defined most usefully as growth in economic activities across national borders at a more rapid rate than growth in national economies, resulting in deeper linkages between national economies and international markets.[3] It is not a new phenomenon, and earlier periods of economic globalization are frequently cited, such as from the latter half of the nineteenth century through 1914 when the ratio of imports to gross domestic product (GDP) attained levels not reached again until the late 1970s or early 1980s. There was, in fact, considerable nineteenth-century commentary on economic globalization, most prominently by the economic determinist Karl Marx, who described the process in his typical class-conscious terms: "The need of a constantly expanding market for its products chases the bourgeoisie over the whole surface of the globe. . . . [National industries] are dislodged by new industries . . . that no longer work up indigenous raw material, but raw material drawn from the remotest zones; industries whose products are consumed, not only at home, but in every quarter of the globe. . . . In place of the old local and national seclusion of self-sufficiency, we have intercourse in every direction, universal interdependence of nations."[4]

A central question at this juncture is thus whether the current surge in international trade and investment, which began in the mid-1980s, is simply one more "wave" of a cyclical pattern, or something new, different, and more consequential than what has come before. Influential observers hold that the current wave is not that exceptional. Professor Paul Krugman, for example, contends that "the importance of international trade to today's U.S. economy is not unprecedented, or even unusual, by historical standards."[5] The World Trade Organization (WTO) Economic Research and Analysis Division concludes, "the rate of increase and the ratio of trade to GDP in the most recent ten-year period (i.e., 1984–94) is more appropriately described not as an acceleration relative to 1974–84, but rather as a return to the rising trend in that ratio evident during the preceding quarter century. . . . A fundamental process of global economic integration was interrupted during 1974–84, after which it got back on track."[6]

The point of analytic departure here is to challenge this view that nothing fundamental has changed in the world economy and to demonstrate that the current wave of economic globalization is both quantitatively and qualitatively different from what has gone before—that a discontinuity from trend has taken place with far-reaching implications for the world political and economic order and for U.S. interests in it. Charles Oman presents the historical context for this view in his study *The Policy Challenges of Globalisation and Regionalisation* in which he describes three distinct waves of economic globalization since the mid-nineteenth century.[7] The first wave, running from 1870 to 1914, involved the high import/GDP ratios cited by Krugman, and was characterized by financial trusts and joint stock companies operating as oligopolies within the more industrialized countries and in their trade relationships elsewhere. England, at the center of the process, imported cotton from the United States, foodstuffs and other raw materials from various sources, and exported textiles and other manufactured products. Comparative advantage relationships were stable and simple to demonstrate. The second wave of postwar economic globalization in the 1950s and the 1960s included the advent of the multinational corporation (MNC) in manufacturing, but with direct investment abroad focused mainly on production or assembly to serve the host country market. Developing countries remained largely suppliers of raw materials and basic foodstuffs, although with significant beginnings for textile and other labor-intensive manufactured exports. Relative cost relationships remained reasonably clear-cut although Europe and

Japan were progressively narrowing the gap with the high-wage, capital- and technology-intensive American economy.

The third wave of economic globalization began in the mid-1980s after a decade of relatively slow growth in international trade and foreign direct investment caused by two oil crises, global recession induced by extraordinarily high interest rates in the United States, and the related Third World debt crisis. Still in full upswing, and probably accelerating in key respects, this third wave has three, mutually reinforcing stimuli, each making this wave highly distinct from the earlier two waves:[8]

1. The Triumph of Economic Liberalism. National markets opened dramatically to increased competition, internally and externally, throughout the 1980s and into the 1990s. The United States took the lead in broad-scale deregulation, followed by the United Kingdom and, more recently, other industrialized countries. Trade liberalization through the multilateral Uruguay Round and regional free trade agreements in Europe and North America continues, with increasing emphasis on the inclusion of regulatory and other trade-related policies within the trading system, in order to achieve full international "contestability" of national markets. The most dramatic change came as developing countries and former and remaining Communist countries reversed long-standing policies of state-run industries and high protection against imports through market reform objectives of privatization, deregulation, and open trade and investment. The net result is a radically changed policy framework, approaching a global scale, strongly conducive to economic globalization.

2. The Information Technology Revolution. The rate of technological change, based on the rapid development of information-based technologies, is truly revolutionary in impact by any historical standard. The beginnings were in the 1950s, with the development of the semiconductor and early computers, but the critical takeoff for commercial application of information technologies affecting international trade and investment only started in the 1980s. Its impact, now pervasive and of growing consequence in virtually all sectors of the economy—manufacturing, agriculture, telecommunications, financial services, transportation, medical services, and education—will increase further due to the recent advent of open internet communications. The net result is to create a dramatically altered set of technical parameters for stimulating new international economic linkages.

3. The Internationalization of Private Sector Enterprise. The combined results of the first two stimuli greatly increases the scope of commercially viable comparative advantage among nations. This scope, because of its dynamic character, is impossible for economists to measure fully but is nevertheless readily apparent to private entrepreneurs in terms of potential for their bottom lines. The international exchange of goods, services, capital, technology, management skills, and labor are all expanding. The leading-edge sectors that are both cause and effect of the globalization process are those which constitute the new infrastructure for trade—financial services, telecommunications, and transportation. These sectors are all highly integrated on a global basis, with greatly reduced costs, characteristics which have become the great facilitators of international trade and investment. One consequence of this internationalization is a strong trend toward vertical integration of production across borders by MNCs. Another consequence is the emergence of a new category of financial entrepreneurs who bring together capital, technology, and management expertise to create internationally based enterprises with varying forms of ownership and control, most prominently for infrastructure projects in the electric power, telecommunications, and transportation sectors, thus reinforcing further the overall globalization process.

That these three interacting stimuli are propelling economic globalization to unprecedented levels is increasingly apparent. This third wave of globalization, moreover, is different and more far-reaching, in functional and geographic terms, than anything that has gone before. The critical questions remain, however, as to how fast and how far the globalization process is going, globally and for the U.S. economy in particular, and what impact it is having on economic performance and other developments at the national level. Unfortunately, the answers at this point are partial at best, as summarized here first in terms of how fast and how far, and then in terms of impact.

Quantitative and Qualitative Dimensions

Measuring cross-border economic activities is a multidimensional challenge, with great variation in the availability of data among the dimensions. Data is most available in greatest detail for trade, less so for foreign direct investment (FDI), and sparse to nonexistent for other key dimensions. This disparity is especially troublesome because of a high degree of inverse relation between the availability of data and the explanatory significance of what is being measured. Trade flows today are largely the consequence rather than the cause of cross-border flows of capital, technology, and management skills, and it is increasingly realized that these latter, nontrade dimensions, interacting or packaged together, provide the underlying momentum for the current wave of economic globalization. But because of the difficulties in measuring them, they tend to get downplayed or ignored compared with readily available trade statistics. The ratio of imports or exports to GDP is by far the most frequently utilized measure of economic globalization, sometimes the only one, while in fact, to an increasing degree, trade can be only the tip of the globalization iceberg.

The presentation here remains captive to the usual manner of measuring economic globalization by category in declining order of data availability, but with appropriate qualitative comment to provide a somewhat more balanced overall assessment. Four broad categories of cross-border economic activity are addressed, which unavoidably include some overlap: trade, FDI, nonequity affiliations, and other cross-border economic activities.

Trade

Trade has been growing much faster than global output since the mid-1980s, both in absolute terms and in comparison with previous decades. The starkest measure, provided by the WTO, is the growth in the volume of merchandise exports compared with global merchandise output. Exports grew at a substantially higher rate in each year from 1985 to 1996, with some acceleration of the differential during the 1990s. The cumulative growth in exports over the eleven-year period was 91 percent, compared with only 27 percent for global output. To compare with earlier decades, the ratio of growth in merchandise trade to global output was 1.4 for 1950–64, 1.6 for 1964–74, 1.2 for 1974–84, and a sharply higher 2.8 for 1984–94.[9] The new wave of economic globalization, at least for merchandise trade and output, is thus far more robust than the earlier postwar experience.

Broadening the measure to include trade in services as well as merchandise, and full GDP rather than merchandise output alone, presents greater measurement problems. Data collection for trade in services began in the 1980s, is collected only on a value basis, and is probably understated to a considerable degree. GDP measurement is a controversial subject, beginning with whether to use the traditional exchange-rate accounting procedure or the more recently utilized purchasing-power-parity (ppp) approach. The most comprehensive trade measure of economic globalization is the trend in the ratio of total trade (i.e., merchandise plus services) to GDP, and again the WTO has estimated this trend, taking into account the various measurement difficulties. Their estimated ratios (i.e., exports plus imports as a share of GDP) jumped from 7 percent to 15 percent over the period 1950–74, increased at a slower rate to 18 percent by 1985, and then accelerated to 23 percent by 1995.[10] Overall, a tripling of trade dependency occurred over a forty-five-year period, with no sign of slowing down.

The U.S. economy has more or less kept pace with this global trend of deepening trade dependency, with an accelerated pace since 1986, triggered by the dollar devaluation beginning that year and a broad-based restructuring of U.S. industry to become more competitive in international markets. The ratio of U.S. imports plus exports of merchandise trade to GDP rose from 7 percent in 1950 to 8 percent in 1970, to 14 percent in 1985, and to 17 percent in 1994. Adding in services trade for 1994 brings the ratio up to 22 percent. Current U.S. trade dependency, however, remains relatively low compared with most other countries. Comparable ratios for 1994 (using the ppp measure for GDP), including services, are Belgium-Luxemburg, 150 percent; Brazil, 17 percent; Canada, 67 percent; China, 45 percent; Germany, 54 percent; Indonesia, 50 percent; Japan, 17 percent; Mexico, 43 percent; South Korea, 61 percent; and the United Kingdom, 54 percent.

This overall sustained—and recently accelerating—increase in trade as a share of global output has two principal structural characteristics which derive from the underlying forces of the new wave of economic globalization, one with respect to the sectoral composition of trade, and the other to geographic distribution.

The sectoral composition of merchandise trade has shifted steadily to a preponderant concentration in manufactured goods. As shown in table 1, the manufactures share of total exports increased from 54 percent in 1963 to 63 percent in 1985 and to 77 percent in 1995, while agricultural products and nonagricultural raw materials were in secular decline to 12 percent and 4 percent, respectively, in 1995. The mineral fuels share declined to less than 10 percent in the 1990s after achieving higher levels through the 1980s as a result of the oil crises of the 1970s. Comparable trend figures for trade in services are not

TABLE 1.1 : Sectoral Share of World Exports of Goods, 1963–1995
(as Percentage of Total Exports)

	1963	1970	1980	1985	1990	1991	1992	1993	1994	1995
1. Manufactures	54	62	55	63	72	74	75	76	77	77
2. Mineral fuels	10	10	25	19	11	10	9	9	8	7
3. Agricultural products	29	21	15	14	13	13	13	12	12	12
4. Nonagricultural raw materials	7	7	5	4	4	3	3	3	3	4

Sources: United Nations, *Monthly Bulletin of Statistics* (New York: 1963–1985); GATT/ WTO, *International Trade Statistics* (Geneva: 1993–1996); WTO, *Annual Report, 1996* (Geneva: 1996).

available, but in 1995 world exports of commercial services totaled $1.2 trillion, compared with $4.7 trillion for merchandise exports. Combining merchandise and services exports for 1995, the sectoral shares were manufactures, 61 percent; services, 20 percent; agriculture, 10 percent; mineral fuels, 6 percent; and nonagricultural raw materials, 3 percent. Manufactures and services together thus accounted for 81 percent of total exports and are clearly the continuing high-growth sectors, which is relevant to the current globalization process in that they are more directly associated with FDI and other nonequity affiliations described below.

The geographic distribution of trade since the 1960s can be characterized as "tripolar" in that it has been concentrated within and among the three industrialized regions of Western Europe, North America, and East Asia. As shown in table 2, this tripolar orientation deepened substantially during the 1980s, with the share of world trade within the three poles increasing from 40 percent to 49 percent and among the poles from 19 percent to 27 percent, while trade with and among all other parts of the world—including South Asia, South America, Africa, the Middle East, and the former Soviet Union—declined from 41 percent to 24 percent. This tripolar concentration appears to have peaked, however, and declined modestly in 1995, reflecting the more truly global scope of trade which is now emerging. There was also a significant shift within the tripolar grouping, with a growing East Asia share offset by a decline for Western Europe. The dominance of the three advanced industrialized regions in world trade will continue, however, for at least another decade and probably longer.

In sum, trade has been growing rapidly since the mid-1980s, concentrated in manufactured products and services as traded within and among the more industrialized regions, and with the United States among the leaders in trade growth. This increase in trade-based globalization to unprecedented levels can only be explained in part, however, by recent reductions in trade barriers and transportation costs. The greater explanation lies in the other dimensions of economic globalization, beginning with FDI.

Foreign Direct Investment (FDI)

Chart 1 tells the story of the extraordinary expansion of FDI beginning in 1986 after a flat to declining trend during the prior 13 years. The initial surge was triggered by the devaluation of the dollar vis-à-vis the yen beginning in 1986, which led, in particular, to a large outflow of Japanese FDI, mostly to the United States. The moderate decline in global FDI in 1991–92 is similarly related to a subsequent falloff in Japanese FDI, but the upward momentum resumed in 1993 and has continued to rise on a much broader geographic basis, reaching $315 billion in 1995, or more than six times the 1985 level in current dollars. The other measure presented in chart 1 shows the ratio of FDI to global GDP. This ratio, which takes account of inflation, shows a

TABLE 1.2 : The Tripolarization of World Trade
(as Percentage of World Imports of Goods)

	1980	1990	1995
1. Within the Three Poles	40.0	49.0	46.4
OECD Europe	28.0	33.0	26.7
North America	5.9	6.5	7.4
East Asia[a]	6.1	9.5	12.3[b]
2. Among the Three Poles	19.4	26.5	25.8
Europe-North America	7.7	8.0	7.0
East Asia-North America	7.1	10.5	11.0
Europe-East Asia	4.6	8.0	7.8
3. All Other	40.6	24.5	27.8

Sources: IMF, *Direction of Trade Statistics Yearbook* (Washington, D.C.: 1981, 1991, 1996); IMF, Direction of Trade Statistics (Washington, D.C.: September 1996); Board of Foreign Trade, *Foreign Trade Development of the Republic of China* (Taiwan: 1996).
a. Japan, South Korea, China, Hong Kong, Taiwan, and ASEAN.
b. Taiwan's import figures for 1995 include only its major trading partners.

CHART 1 : FDI Outflows and as Share of Global GDP
(1975–95)

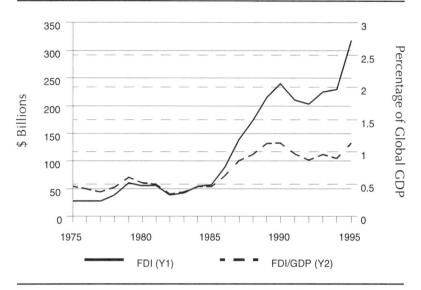

FDI (Y1)   FDI/GDP (Y2)

Sources: FDI: UNCTAD; internal sources; UN, *World Investment Report* (Geneva: 1991–96). GDP: World Bank; internal sources; World Bank, *World Tables* (Washington, D.C.: 1995).

downward trend through 1983, with FDI on the order of 0.4 percent of GDP, and then a near tripling to over 1 percent in 1995.

Data on FDI has many shortcomings, including limited availability and problems of definition. For example, FDI is defined as an enterprise that controls assets of entities in countries other than its home country, usually by owning an equity capital stake of 10 percent or more. FDI flow and stock levels are calculated as the sum of equity capital purchased, reinvested earnings (in proportion to equity participation), and intracompany loans and debt transactions. The full scope of economic activity controlled by FDI affiliates is thus considerably larger than recorded FDI stock and flow levels, in some cases several times larger, but data is not available on such an aggregate basis.

In any event, the recent rapid FDI expansion has resulted in increasing attention to assessing FDI flows. The United Nations Conference on Trade and Development (UNCTAD) annual *World Investment Report* is a widely read, valuable source for this information. Another important source is the WTO secretariat's October 1996 evaluation, "Trade and Foreign Direct Investment," which focuses on interlinkages between FDI and world trade. The starting empirical points for such a focus are that sales of foreign affiliates of multinational corporations (MNCs)—over $6 trillion in 1995—exceed the value of world trade in goods and services, and that an estimated one-third of world trade consists of MNC intrafirm trade and another third consists of MNC exports to nonaffiliates. The combination of FDI and the operations of MNCs has thus clearly become a central driving force for economic globalization in terms of domestic sales of affiliates and of trade creation.

Detailed assessment of how this driving force operates is more limited, although some characteristics are apparent. FDI in mining and other natural-resource-based industries tends to follow a relatively straight-forward and sequential pattern of stimulating initial imports of machinery and equipment in the host country, which then leads to sustained exports of the resource material. The FDI/trade relationship is more varied and complex for manufacturing and service industries, with information on the services sector being particularly sparse. There are clear examples of "tariff-jumping," whereby FDI circumvents import protection and substitutes for trade, such as the Japanese automotive transplants in the United States in the 1980s and pharmaceutical sector FDI throughout the developing world. There is also an important distinction between MNC vertical integration, whereby lower-cost activities—usually labor—are sourced abroad through FDI, and horizontal integration, whereby MNCs establish production abroad for sales in foreign markets, taking advantage of experience with more advanced technology application, superior management/organizational capability, and the spreading of research and development costs. In both categories, available studies indicate that FDI can lead to a net increase in trade, but often with significant change in its composition. The 1996 WTO evaluation states, "Empirical research suggests that to the extent there is a systemic relationship between FDI and home-country exports, it is positive but not very pronounced. . . . There is less evidence on the relationship between FDI and home country imports, but what exists tends to suggest a positive but weak relationship."[11]

The uneven geographic distribution of FDI is even more striking than that of trade, and also subject to a faster pace of change. In 1990, FDI by and among the advanced industrialized countries—Western Europe, the United States, Canada, Japan, and Australia/New Zealand—constituted 93 percent of global outflows of FDI and 83 percent of inflows.[12] One glaring asymmetry in the balance of FDI flows was Japan, which accounted for 22 percent of the outflow of the grouping but only 1 percent of the inflow. FDI has generally not been welcome in Japan, a sentiment being imitated by South Korea, where the recent increase in FDI outflow by Korean "chaebol" industrial conglomerates stands in contrast to the persistent low level of FDI inflow.

Most other emerging economies of Asia, Latin America, and Central and Eastern Europe, however, have been rapidly growing recipients of FDI. By 1995, the shares of global FDI by and among the industrialized grouping had dropped to 85 percent of outflows and 64 percent of inflows. In absolute terms, FDI flows to developing (including former/remaining communist) countries increased steadily from $13 billion in 1985 to $34 billion in 1990, and to $100 billion in 1995.

Two noteworthy dimensions of this rapid increase in FDI to developing countries concern the least-developed grouping of countries and China. The poorest, least-developed countries are by definition poor environments for investment, and they have been almost totally excluded from the southward surge of FDI, receiving less than 1 percent of the total flow. While relatively numerous in terms of countries—sixty according to the World Bank definition of "IDA-only" countries eligible for soft loans from the International Development Association—these poorest countries nevertheless constitute only a relatively small 16 percent share of the total population of developing countries. Developing countries with the remaining 84 percent of the population are by and large benefiting from the recent globalization of FDI.

China has been the largest and most spectacularly growing recipient of FDI, with inflows rising ten-fold from $3.5 billion in 1990 to $37.5 billion in 1995, much of it coming from Taiwan via Hong Kong. China is not, however, as disproportionately represented as sometimes is depicted. The rate of increase of FDI to China in 1994 and 1995 was slower than it was to other developing countries, and this trend is likely to continue. In 1995, China accounted for 38 percent of FDI to developing countries while representing 28 percent of the total developing country population, or 33 percent of the population excluding the nonengaged least-developed countries.

FDI, in conclusion, is a rapidly growing dimension of economic globalization and a central force for growth in trade, in the process becoming truly globalized in scope except for the least-developed grouping of countries. More qualitative questions about its evolving structure and relationship to trade, critical for projecting the future course of globalization, have less clear answers. For example, to what extent is FDI in the form of cross-border vertical integration—in particular, as a process of outsourcing labor-intensive operations to low-wage countries—a one-time adjustment to the new circumstances of more open markets and lower transportation/communications costs which may be peaking out or even reversing in some sectors? Direct labor costs as a share of total manufacturing costs fell by more than half from the mid-1970s to the late 1980s, and now account for as little as 10 percent of total costs for standardized auto parts and 2 percent for semiconductors. Oman raises more far-reaching questions regarding what he sees as a fundamental shift from relatively fixed, "one best way" production of goods and services to "flexible production" in terms of "continuous innovation in the way things are done, as well as in what is produced."[13] The current outlook for the international telecommunications sector would be a good case in point for analyzing such flexible production. All of these questions, moreover, demonstrate the fading line that can be drawn between FDI and "nonequity affiliations."

Nonequity affiliations

An FDI is defined in terms of a minimum share of equity ownership and FDI flows and stocks are calculated on such an equity-ownership basis. Other forms of cross-border enterprise relationships are also important, however, indeed of growing importance within the new wave of economic globalization, and are addressed here as "nonequity affiliations." Unfortunately, basic data about such relationships are even more sparse than for FDI, especially in the services sector which is particularly prominent in this area. The 1996 United Nations Conference on Trade and Development (UNCTAD) investment report concludes simply: "Little is known about the trade impact of services TNCs [transnational corporations]."[14] What follows is thus a mostly descriptive summary of three principal categories of nonequity affiliations:

   1. Infrastructure. MNCs are becoming increasingly engaged in infrastructure projects (principally in the transportation, electric power, and telecommunications sectors), but only a small part of it is recorded as FDI. In 1992, a mere 3 percent of total foreign assets of U.S. affiliates was in infrastructure, although this share is growing, particularly in telecommunications. In developing countries, privatization of infrastructure provides opportunities for FDI, but this, too, remains limited in scope—about $5 billion in 1995—compared with projected financial requirements for infrastructure over the coming decade of $1.4 trillion in East Asia and $600–800 billion in Latin America alone. The primary vehicles for infrastructure project development and finance in developing countries are non- or minimum-equity affiliations, including build-own-operate (BOO), build-operate-transfer (BOT), and build-transfer-operate (BTO) arrangements. The international enterprise, or more frequently a team of enterprises, generally seeks to minimize direct financial participation, and the financial package centers on official export finance (since imports constitute a major component of infrastructure projects), multilateral development bank and host government financing, bond flotations, and commercial bank loans. Twenty-seven billion dollars in loans and bonds were recorded in 1995, and total infrastructure financing, domestic and international, was clearly much larger. The critical contribution of the MNCs is the capability to organize, construct, and manage technology-intensive infrastructure projects far more efficiently than the host government or national enterprises, and, through this capability, to attract the necessary financing and to negotiate with the host government a regulatory and other policy framework adequate to make the project commercially viable.

2. Service Sector Franchise and Management Contracts. These are especially prominent in the hotel, restaurant, fast food, and car rental services sectors. In developing countries, they can form the core of a burgeoning tourism sector, with links to air and sea transportation services. For Caribbean island economies (except Cuba), for example, tourism revenues are now more than six times larger than sugar, coffee, and banana exports combined, largely carried out through cross-border franchise and management contracts. Even in Cuba, the recent expansion of hotel and related tourist services has been developed primarily on a management contract basis rather than through FDI. Such franchise and management contract relationships have existed for a long time, but the recent proliferation is directly related to the rapid expansion and cost reduction in international communications and transportation—in other words, a third wave globalization effect.

3. Other Marketing and Long-term Contract Arrangements. Many goods producing sectors also involve long-term international marketing and production contract relationships. A wide range of consumer goods production is marketed through retail chains operated on an international basis. Nontraditional agricultural products—fruits, vegetables, and flowers—particularly in developing countries, are likewise marketed globally through contracts which include quality controls and brand-name labeling. Much of the assembly industry in developing countries is also carried out on a long-term contract basis rather than through equity investment by the parent company. Again, all of these forms of cross-border company relationships have been around for decades if not centuries, but the application in recent years of new technologies to marketing and transportation has enabled an unprecedented and continuing expansion.

A distinguishing characteristic of these nonequity affiliations compared with FDI is that they can be organized and put into operation relatively quickly. The MNC does not have to ponder a large high-risk up-front commitment of investment capital—as with FDI by definition—and can thus react promptly to a proposed project. Private infrastructure providers remember the wave of nationalizations in the 1960s and1970s and are far more disposed to proceed when they have only a minimal direct financial stake. Multilateral hotel and food distribution companies would also be much more hesitant to move ahead in these sectors if they had to make large equity commitments in buildings and agricultural property development that could later be held financial hostage by host governments.

The flip side of this more rapid deployment of nonequity affiliation investment projects is that they are also more volatile in terms of quicker termination if the investment climate in the host country turns negative. Implementation of infrastructure projects can stall, hotel franchise owners can go bankrupt, and assembly operations can be shifted rapidly to other, more hospitable host country environments. Another Caribbean example is the flourishing assembly industry in Haiti of the 1980s. Over 200 companies in the textile, electronics, footwear, toys, and sporting goods sectors—built up over two decades, mostly on a long-term contract basis—shut down abruptly and moved elsewhere in the early 1990s as a result of the international embargo and political instability.

Other Cross-border Economic Activities

There are many other forms of cross-border economic activities, beyond trade, FDI, and nonequity affiliations as discussed thus far, also taking on new and expanded forms of globalization. They can only be addressed here in briefest form, most conveniently in terms of the factors of production: investment, technology, and labor.

   1. Investment. The discussion of the international flow of investment capital has been limited to direct equity investments (FDI) and international financial packages organized through nonequity affiliations. Another major and growing source of cross-border investment capital is portfolio investment facilitated by the information-technology-based globalization of capital markets. The international flow of portfolio investment totaled about $500 billion in 1995, of which over $50 billion went to developing countries. The United States has substantial two-way traffic in portfolio investment, with $44 billion of net outflows and $99 billion of net inflows recorded in 1995. The other principal category of international long-term capital flow is official development finance to developing countries, principally from multilateral development banks, but this has remained about level since the early 1980s and is of declining relative importance. In 1995, according to the World Bank, the total net capital flow to developing countries was $231 billion, of which $90 billion was FDI, $56 billion was portfolio investment, and only $12.5 billion, or about 5 percent, was multilateral development bank loans.[15]

   2. Technology. Most cross-border transfer of technology takes place within FDI and nonequity affiliation projects, wherein new technologies are directly applied in foreign productive enterprises. Other forms of technology transfer include licensing, theft, and free access. Royalty and licensing fees produced payments of $27 billion to U.S. firms in 1995, up sharply from about $4–7 million per year in the late 1970s and early 1980s, while theft of technology through violation of intellectual property rights is estimated to cost U.S. companies more than $40 billion per year. Freely available technology comes largely from public research laboratories, most prominently in the agricultural sector, and its application in developing countries is facilitated by economic aid projects and technical assistance.

3. Labor. It is often assumed that labor is not mobile across borders because of the constraints of immigration policies, but this is only partially true in quantitative terms and even more misleading in qualitative terms. The international movement of unskilled labor is severely restricted in most countries, but relatively large numbers of illegal immigrants and temporary workers do cross borders with significant impact on host economies, including the U.S. economy, and even greater impact on poor home countries through remittance payments from workers abroad. Of high qualitative importance is the growing international flow of managers and other professionals that form an integral and often critical component of FDI and other investment projects. Facilitating such professional labor movement has been addressed in the Uruguay Round services agreement, the North American Free Trade Agreement (NAFTA), and Asia-Pacific Economic Cooperation (APEC) discussions. Yet another qualitatively important category is the cross-border labor flow of students at the university level, with the U.S. university system playing the central role. Approximately 270,000 foreign students are enrolled as undergraduates and another 180,000 as graduate students in U.S. universities. It is a two-stage labor flow, with the first, student stage largely an international services sector transaction whereby the U.S. university provides education services for cross-border payment (although it is a highly subsidized international service, particularly in public universities). The second stage is more clearly a long-term cross-border migration with a highly positive impact on economic performance. Foreign graduates that remain in the United States, especially in science and engineering, contribute significantly to technology-intensive U.S. industries, while those that return home often play prominent public and private sector leadership roles.[16]

This brief summary of the various dimensions of the current wave of economic globalization demonstrates, if nothing else, the broad scope and pervasive character of what is happening. Measurement problems have been noted at various points, especially for relating the different components. The integration problem carries over to economic theory and model building which, while not addressed here, is a subject of growing interest for economists. Theoretical work on trade and FDI, for example, was carried out on largely separate tracks until the 1980s, and

TABLE 1.3: Third Wave Globalization: Indicators of a Discontinuity
since the Mid-1980s

	Before	After
1. Ratio of growth in merchandise trade to global output	1.2–1.6 (1950–84)	2.8 (1984–94)
2. FDI as a percent of global GDP	0.4–0.6 (1970–85)	0.9–1.2 (1990–95)
3. Royalty and licensing fees to U.S. companies	$4 billion (1975) $7 billion (1980) $7 billion (1985)	$17 billion (1990) $27 billion (1995)
4. Foreign exchange transactions, daily	$10–20 billion (1973) $60 billion (1983)	$700 billion (1990) $1.3 trillion (1995)
5. International telephone calls to and from the U.S (in minutes)	500 million (1975) 3 billion (1980) 6 billion (1985)	12 billion (1990) 23 billion (1995)

Sources: Merchandise Trade: WTO, *International Trade: Trends and Statistics* (Geneva: 1995). FDI: World Bank; internal sources; World Bank, *World Tables* (Washington D.C.: 1995); UNCTAD; UN, *World Investment Report* (Geneva: 1991–96). Royalty and Licensing Fees: Bureau of Economic Analysis, *Survey of Current Business* (Washinton D.C.: U.S. Department of Commerce, July 1996). Foreign Exchange: Bank for International Settlements, *Central Bank Survey of Foreign Exchange and Derivatives Market Activities* (Basel: BIS, 1995); The Economist Intelligence Unit, "Survey of the World Economy", in *The Economist*, 7–13 October 1995, 63. International Telephone Calls: Federal Communications Commission, *U.S. International Trends Report* (Washington D.C.: 1996); internal sources.

recent work to integrate the two is still of limited utility.[17] Integrating the broader aspects of international capital, technology, and labor flows is even more daunting in theoretical as well as measurement terms.

The central question remains, however, whether the available information is sufficient to demonstrate a marked discontinuity in the globalization trend of the past half-century, indicating a new phase beginning in the mid-1980s, more robust quantitatively and more pervasive qualitatively than previous years—in short, a distinctive third wave. The case for such a discontinuity is supported by the indicators presented in table 3. The first three—concerning trade, FDI, and technology transfer in terms of royalty and licensing fees—were cited earlier in the text. The final two—foreign exchange transactions and cross border telephone calls—are proxies for financial and telecommunications services, the new information-based infrastructure for international trade and investment. Although these five indicators do not tell the whole story (additional indicators can and hopefully will be developed over time), a reasonably convincing case for the recognition of a new and distinct third wave of economic globalization clearly emerges.[18]

A final comment that forms a bridge to the subsequent sections on U.S. interests concerns the unprecedented geographic scope of the current globalization process, within a "one-four-one" configuration. The impact of the current globalization process is distinct among three population groupings: approximately one billion people in the advanced industrialized countries, four billion in the newly emerging market economies (of which China and India represent almost half), and one billion in the poorest countries, who, temporarily at least, are being left behind. The fastest economic growth, driven largely by globalization, is taking place within the emerging market four billion grouping. Average annual growth in GDP for all developing countries rose to 4 percent in 1990–93 and to 6 percent in 1994–96—double that of the industrialized· grouping—and this differential is expected to continue at least through the end of the decade. This is a sharply different picture from the uneven and generally disappointing growth performance of developing countries during the 1960s and 1970s and the Third World debt crisis of the early 1980s. It also presents a new and far different context for assessing U.S. interests in economic globalization.

The Impact on Economic Growth and Productivity

The following assessment of the impact of economic globalization on U.S. interests begins with "gains from trade," that is, the increase in economic growth and productivity at the national level deriving from the globalization process. The unambiguously positive findings here are followed by consideration of the more mixed impact of globalization on economic adjustment and national sovereignty/security.

The classic gains from trade in goods, based on comparative advantage, are familiar and easy to demonstrate: England exports textiles to Portugal, imports wine in return, and consumers in both countries benefit. The benefits, moreover, lend themselves to measurement based on the relative costs of production in the two countries. The highly dynamic context of third wave economic globalization, however, presents a vastly more complex challenge of concept and measurement, while at the same time yielding a far broader range of economic gains. The term "gains from trade," in fact, is misleadingly narrow, and should be recast as the gains from international trade, investment, and other cross-border economic activities.

The starting point for assessing the economic gains from globalization is to admit that there is no way to make a precise measurement of the full gains obtained. The best that can be done, as presented here, is to estimate a first tier of gains that can be measured with some precision, to provide a more approximate estimate for a second tier of recognizable gains, and then to make a mostly descriptive statement about the third and possibly most important tier of gains that defies quantitative measurement. From this cumulative process, and following the Keynesian admonition that "it is better to be roughly right than precisely wrong," an overall, heavily judgmental net assessment can be made about the impact of globalization on U.S. economic growth and productivity.

The measurable first tier of economic benefits from increased trade concerns the "static" gains resulting from differences in relative costs of production among countries, as described in the England/Portugal relationship above. Based on estimated price elasticities of demand, calculations can be made of the increase in national income and productivity from a given increase in trade. An estimate by the GATT secretariat, for example, of such gains from trade due to Uruguay Round trade liberalization indicated an increase of 23 percent in the global volume of merchandise exports, resulting in an increase of about .5 percent in world income, or $184 billion, by 2005.[19] These estimates have some downward bias and do not include trade in services, but the increase in world income would probably remain less than 1 percent after ten years. U.S. trade in recent years has grown much more than 23 percent, the volume of merchandise exports doubling from 1986 to 1995, thus producing a considerably larger but still relatively modest increase in economic growth on this basis, on the order of two- to three-tenths of a percent per year.

A major problem of public perception about the gains from trade is that economic reporting, as well as economic analysis by professional economists, often stops at this point of relatively clear and quantitative conclusions. Such reporting and analysis, however, falls victim to being "precisely wrong," because it ignores the far more important yet elusive "dynamic gains from trade."[20] Recently, greater attention has been paid to these dynamic gains—gains involving changes in what and how goods and services are produced as a result of more open markets—but the inherent problems of identifying and measuring them have limited quantifiable results thus far. The dynamic trade effects, in fact, can further be divided between those that have been estimated in quantitative terms, albeit with somewhat heroic assumptions, and those that remain beyond any means of quantification, referred to here, respectively, as the second and third tier gains.

The same GATT study of trade effects from Uruguay Round liberalization analyzed second tier, dynamic effects concerning economies of scale and imperfect competition for existing industries and estimated a total world income growth effect of $510 billion—almost two and a half times that of the static trade effects alone. This is consistent with other assessments which claim dynamic trade effects to be two to three times larger than the static effects.[21]

Possibly even more important, however, are the third tier economic gains that are beyond the scope of economic models based on a relatively fixed existing structure of production and trade. The GATT trade study, for example, does not take account of the economic impact of new investment projects and the introduction of new technologies across borders induced by the Uruguay Round agreement. A basic restructuring of existing industries in response to new international competition—especially for technology-intensive industries such as telecommunications and financial services—would also fall outside existing measurement practices. And yet these third tier dynamic economic gains go to the heart of much of the current economic globalization process.

At this point, the most that can be done about such third tier dynamic effects is to cite some prominent examples and to urge that economists give greater analytic attention to the subject. Telecommunications and financial services have already been noted, and the services sector in general deserves greater prominence. Other examples of large third tier dynamic effects from economic globalization include:

1. The U.S. Automotive Sector. The surge of imported automobiles, mainly from Japan, which resulted in a rise in imports from 18 percent of U.S. consumption in 1977 to 27 percent in 1987, created enormous pressures for U.S. industry to undertake a broad-based restructuring. When Japanese companies shifted from export of finished automobiles to FDI in transplant production in the United States (basically a tariff-jumping, or more precisely a voluntary-export-restraint-jumping, effect), the competitive pressures on U.S. firms increased further. As a result, U.S. firm productivity rose dramatically. Labor output in the U.S. automotive sector rose almost 4 percent per year during the 1980s, while the quality differential between U.S. and Japanese cars narrowed greatly. Assigning a precise share of these extraordinary improvements to gains from trade cannot be done, but the first tier static gains would be limited to the lower cost of the 27 percent of imported cars for consumers, and these gains would actually decline to the extent that imported vehicles are replaced by transplant production by Japanese companies. The full gains would have to include not only the lower cost and higher quality of the 70 plus percent of U.S. firm automobile sales induced by the surge of imports and FDI, but also growth in sales by U.S. affiliates in foreign markets caused, for example, by lower cost U.S. firm production in Europe vis-à-vis European competitors.

2. *Pentium, Windows, and* Jurassic Park. These three high visibility U.S. products share the characteristic of high initial investment and development costs followed by a very low to minimal cost for production of the actual product. In other words, the economies of scale are enormous compared with manufacturing industry in general, and this leads to extremely large dynamic gains from trade as these products are marketed abroad. In addition to the resulting high profit margins, which can be used for investment in new products, the prices of these products to consumers tend to fall, at home and abroad. The share of Intel sales outside the United States in 1996, largely Pentium chips, was 58 percent, or $12 billion. A similar share of Microsoft software was sold abroad, or $4.7 billion, as was 60 percent of *Jurassic Park*'s cumulative box office sales, about $550 million. The large majority of these foreign sales can be taken as a rough approximation of the combined static and dynamic gains from trade for these prominent U.S. export products.

3. *The Philippines under President Fidel Ramos.* The newly emerging market economies in Asia, Latin America, and Central Europe are clearly the largest potential beneficiaries of economic globalization as they rapidly and broadly open their markets to international competition and to the other dimensions of globalization. They also have greater scope for improvement in terms of a once-over adjustment to productivity levels

in industrialized countries. The transformation of the Philippine economy, under the economic reform program of President Ramos from 1992 to 1996 is a striking case in point. The Philippine economic growth rate was near zero in 1992 and increased steadily to 6–7 percent by 1996, with projections to remain on a high growth path if market opening reforms continue to move ahead. Export growth of over 20 percent a year led the expansion and FDI tripled from $500 million to $1.5 billion per year. Duty-free export zones increased from one to eighteen. Deregulation and privatization of electric power, telecommunications, and financial services, allowing for participation and competition from foreign advanced-technology companies, was critical for the overall economic success by eliminating bottlenecks in vital infrastructure. The question is how much of this zero to 6–7 percent growth takeoff can be attributed to the effects of international market-oriented reforms and the resulting economic globalization. One could easily assign half-credit, or perhaps credit for almost all of the growth since, without the reforms and related exports and FDI, the Philippines would likely have remained the zero growth "sick man of Asia" rather than an aspiring new Asian "tiger" economy.

These are the various elements of positive impact on growth and productivity from economic globalization. Adding them together requires a much less than fully-informed judgment, but it is nevertheless a critical judgment. For the U.S. economy, are the incremental gains from globalization merely two- or three-tenths of a percent of economic growth per year, or are they much larger, perhaps as much as 1 percent or more? It is irresponsible to avoid a judgmental answer by getting it precisely wrong. We have to do our best to get it roughly right.

Before venturing a roughly right answer, however, it is necessary to consider one other deeply integrated dimension of the trade performance picture, namely, the overall course of the U.S. economy. The U.S. national economy is going through a restructuring process similar to that of the international economy, largely driven by technological change and industrial reorganization. This has led to large gains in productivity for manufacturing industry, officially measured at over 3 percent per year since the mid-1980s, but the picture is less clear for the now dominant services sector, which employs three-quarters of the labor force. Any judgment on the impact of international economic activities on national economic performance, however, needs to be related to the aggregate rates of growth in economic output and productivity. This leads to what has been an apparent paradox of decisive importance.

The apparent paradox is between the implied very substantial gains from international trade and investment described above, however imprecise the measurement of the dynamic effects, and the longstanding assessed growth in U.S. productivity of only about 1 percent per year over the past twenty years. This gloomy domestic economic outlook has been consistently reported by reputable observers. For example, the September 1996 report of the Competitiveness Policy Council, *Running in Place: Recent Trends in U.S. Living Standards,* includes such findings as, "The median family income after inflation in 1993 ($36,959) was only marginally higher than it was in 1973 ($36,893). . . . Wage declines over the last 20 years have resulted in stagnant incomes and a deterioration in the distribution of income for all but the wealthiest 5 percent of the population." But if overall national economic performance is characterized by declining incomes for 95 percent of the population, how can the international sector, which in any event constitutes a relatively small share of the total, contribute anything more than a very small offsetting positive effect? Put another way, if the international gains were substantial—on the order of 1 percent per year of additional GDP growth and a corresponding significant contribution to productivity growth—the performance of the remainder of the economy would be so anemic as to be implausible even to the most pessimistic observers.

The explanation of this apparent paradox, fortunately, is that it has been without merit. The statistical underpinnings are incorrect, which has led to widespread understatement of U.S. economic performance. The fact is that U.S. wages, family incomes, and productivity, taking *full* account of inflation, have been growing at a relatively brisk pace over the past twenty years. The principal problem stems from the persistent use of a faulty consumer price index (CPI) and related indices to adjust for inflation. The majority of economists who have examined the methodology for constructing the CPI believe that it overstates the rate of inflation, probably by more than 1 percent per year. If the CPI is adjusted by 1–1.5 percent to approximate the true rate of inflation, the increase in U.S. wages plus benefits from 1975 to 1995 would increase from a meager 2 percent to 25–35 percent. The annual growth in GDP would likewise rise from 2–2.5 percent to over 3 percent per year, and the international sector could more plausibly be making a substantial contribution to this more buoyant economic performance.

The consequences of an overstated CPI are receiving belated attention as a result of the Boskin Commission report,[22] but mainly for its budget implications—the higher entitlement and lower tax payments resulting from an overstated CPI—while the broader implications for economic growth and productivity still tend to be downplayed. One reason for this disregard is that both major political parties use the issue of stagnant wage levels to their targeted advantage—the Democrats to decry the growing disparity in incomes and the Republicans to bemoan low economic growth during a Democratic presidency. Another reason is the convenience and habit of almost all observers to cite official statistics on growth and income trends despite the fact that the statistics do not fully adjust for inflation.

The conclusion drawn here, however, is that the growth in U.S. economic output and productivity, when full account is taken of inflation, is considerably higher than officially recognized, which, in turn, has international implications in terms of the plausible growth impact of economic globalization. The consequent "roughly right" approximation of the gains to the U.S. economy from current globalization is that these gains are substantial, much larger than generally perceived, and probably add on the order of 1 percent annual growth of GDP and a corresponding increase in productivity.

The Economic Adjustment Impact

In addition to the unambiguously positive "gains from trade," economic globalization entails adjustments in the U.S. economy which can have adverse as well as positive effects on individual segments of the economy and overall performance. Such effects involve the labor force, the structure of industry, the aggregate level of investment, and the balance of external accounts.

The Impact on Labor

The most widely discussed adjustment issue is the impact of globalization on U.S. jobs. The adverse consequences for workers displaced by imports or by outsourcing of production from the United States to foreign plants benefiting from low wages receive continuing political and media attention from critics of a liberal trade policy. Protectionist demagogues make it an all-encompassing issue, epitomized by Ross Perot's "great sucking sound" of U.S. jobs lost to cheap Mexican labor as a result of NAFTA. Some adjustments in the composition of the U.S. labor force are inevitable as a consequence of expanding international trade and investment, but the extent of the trade-induced adjustment can be greatly exaggerated, and the fact that the overall adjustment produces net benefits for U.S. workers can be lost.

The extent of trade-induced job losses are in fact very small compared with overall changes continually taking place in the U.S. labor force. Two million jobs per year have been added to the U.S. economy during the 1990s, and approximately four to five million Americans change their jobs in a given year, largely as a result of new technology applications and industrial restructuring at the national level. By contrast, only about 10,000–20,000 workers per year have qualified for trade adjustment assistance in recent years, wherein imports have been found to be a major factor in job loss. U.S. manufactured imports from developing countries, which are the focus of concern about low-wage foreign competition, totaled $191 billion in 1995, or less than 3 percent of GDP, and such imports from Mexico were $36 billion, or 0.5 percent of GDP.[23]

Moreover, such gross losses in jobs from imports and outward FDI need to be related to job creation from exports and inward FDI. The overriding positive consideration in this relation is that export jobs are more productive, paying on average 13 percent more than other jobs, and the pay gap is even greater for the unskilled jobs most vulnerable to import competition. Since the increases in exports and imports in recent years have been comparable, the net effect on jobs from economic globalization has been roughly neutral. The persistent trade deficit since 1980 does produce a small net adverse effect on total employment that needs to be offset elsewhere in the economy, but the current full employment level for the overall U.S. economy indicates that this has been accomplished.

One other effect of globalization on U.S. labor is a tendency to increase income inequality through downward wage pressure for unskilled jobs, although the degree of such an effect is subject to diverse views by economists. An exhaustive study by William Cline comes out somewhere in the middle, concluding that for the period 1973–93, "suppression of manufactured imports from developing countries would have raised real unskilled wages directly by 4.5 percent, but reduced them indirectly by 3 percent because of higher import costs. The net gain of 1.5 percent would have been small."[24]

In sum, the impact on U.S. jobs from economic globalization is relatively small, with the creation of higher paying export jobs roughly offsetting job losses in import competing industries. Individual workers who are displaced are, of course, interim losers, whether the job loss is from domestic or international sources, and retraining and skill upgrading for all displaced workers—as well as low wage, unskilled workers in general—should be a higher priority for public and private sector resources. The charge that economic globalization is causing serious and widespread harm to the U.S. labor force, however, is unjustified, and public perceptions of the extent of job displacement caused by imports tends to be greatly exaggerated.

The Impact on Industry

The international trade and investment impact on U.S. firms is similar in concept to that on labor, with displacement of some plants or firms by foreign competition offset by new opportunities in export-oriented sectors. There has been less public attention paid to the adverse effects on business, in part because private investors knowingly take risks in the hope of financial rewards, and thus deserve the consequences, be they profits or losses. There is also the broadly acknowledged beneficial result of a more competitive economy from increased foreign competition. In any event, as in the case of labor, only a very small share of the approximately 80,000 firms that go out of business each year in the United States do so because of foreign competition.

The principal concern about the impact of economic globalization on U.S. industrial structure has been the possible decline of advanced technology industries, with broader negative implications for the future development of the U.S. economy, as exemplified by sharply growing Japanese competition in the semiconductor industry in the mid-1980s. This concern, however, has diminished in the 1990s as U.S. firms have regained competitive strength and a preeminent market position in a wide range of technology-intensive industries, including the computer, semiconductor, software, telecommunications, and biotechnology sectors. Since the mid-1980s, increased attention has also been given to policies which support new technology development and application in the United States—such as protection of intellectual property rights, research and development and investment tax benefits, and publicly supported basic research—and reduce trade-distorting industrial policies abroad. As a consequence, the net impact of globalization on U.S. industries, and on advanced technology industry in particular, is viewed in an increasingly favorable light as market growth abroad exceeds that of the domestic economy.

The Impact on Aggregate Investment

In theory, a more open world economy could be expected to result in a net flow of savings from the higher income, more capital-intensive economies to poorer countries where savings rates are presumably lower and returns on capital higher. The United States, as a "mature creditor nation," would experience a net outflow of capital and would receive a progressively higher income from abroad in terms of profits and interest payments on foreign assets. At the same time, the consequent lower level of savings for investment at home would raise the domestic cost of capital slightly and have an inhibiting effect on domestic economic growth.

In fact, while this model roughly approximated the U.S. position in the world economy in the postwar period through 1980, a sharp reversal has occurred since the early 1980s whereby the United States has shifted from being the largest net creditor country—with net assets abroad of about $400 billion in 1980—to the largest net debtor country—with a net debt of one trillion dollars by the end of 1997. What this means for aggregate investment and growth is a complex question and relates to the purpose of the foreign borrowing. Borrowing for productive investment that would not otherwise have taken place results in a positive net effect on growth, even after paying service on the debt abroad. Foreign borrowing for current consumption, in contrast, has the negative consequence of creating an ongoing foreign debt service obligation without any offsetting positive growth.

With respect to FDI, where the relation between foreign debt and productive investment is most direct, the trend over the past 15 years does not follow the overall sharp reversal in U.S. external capital accounts. The net FDI position of the United States (i.e., the stock of equity assets held abroad by U.S. firms minus the stock of such assets held by foreign firms in the United States) declined from $270 billion in 1980 to $171 billion in 1993, and then increased to $216 billion in 1995—an upward trend expected to continue. The limited conclusion that can thus be drawn is that factors other than FDI have acted to make the United States the largest (and continually growing) international debtor nation, and to the extent that this is considered an adverse effect of globalization, a broader examination of the balance of international accounts is in order.

The Impact on the Balance of International Accounts

Economic globalization during the 1990s stimulated a rapid increase in the U.S. foreign debt position through a sharply higher rate of dollar purchases by foreign central banks, from $23 billion per year in the 1980s to $100 billion per year in the 1990s. There are two reasons for this effect. First, the accelerated growth in trade from globalization raises the "prudent level" of foreign central bank reserve holdings, predominantly dollars. Second, the uneven response of governments to globalization has led some of them to a "mercantilist motivation" wherein their central banks buy dollars in order to maintain an undervalued currency vis-à-vis the dollar. This motivation appears evident, for example, in the cases of Japan, China, and Hong Kong, whose combined official purchases of dollars exceeded $200 billion from 1992 to 1996, while reserve holdings in each case were far above any reasonably prudent level. The net result is that almost all of the $600 billion increase in the U.S. foreign debt during the 1990s is directly attributable to dollar purchases by central banks abroad, and much if not all of the remainder of the debt buildup is caused indirectly by the official dollar purchases through the resulting stronger dollar and consequent increase in the U.S. trade deficit. The impact of this continuing large growth in the foreign debt on the U.S. economy is complex. The effects of the growing debt service payments to foreign holders of U.S. debt, including foreign central banks, are largely adverse. A broader question is whether the foreign debt eventually will reach the point where the creditworthiness of dollar-denominated financial instruments will be brought into question, resulting in at least a higher interest rate to service the debt and perhaps more fundamental problems for the dollar-based international financial system.[25]

In conclusion, the adjustment effects of globalization on the U.S. economy are modest and only a small part of the integral and much broader restructuring taking place within the overall

national economy. Labor is clearly the most sensitive and important area for adjustment assistance, and retraining of workers as
part of a comprehensive national strategy to strengthen the U.S.
educational system should be a high national priority. In relative
terms, however, labor adjustment from imports and FDI abroad
is relatively small and offset by the creation of new and higher
paying jobs from growth in exports and FDI into the United
States. The other disturbing adjustment effect of globalization is
the continued rapid growth of the U.S. foreign debt position,
which may require a revised structure for international reserve
holdings.

The Impact on National Sovereignty/Security

The third category of U.S. interests, the impact of economic globalization on U.S. national sovereignty/security, could be the
most important of all, especially if projected out beyond the
short- to medium-term policy horizon, five to ten years, to
several decades or more. This category is also the most complex
and least amenable to precise analysis. The discussion here is
limited to raising six central issues and providing a few broad
lines of assessment and some tentative conclusions.

WTO/NAFTA and U.S. Sovereignty

The Uruguay Round agreement, which created the WTO, and
NAFTA have been the lightning rods for protectionists and neo-
isolationists decrying the loss of U.S. sovereignty due to
economic globalization. However, while these two agreements
constitute major steps for broadening and strengthening the liberal international trading system, their significance in terms of
limitations on U.S. sovereignty has been greatly exaggerated.
Any international agreement acts as a limit on sovereignty as the
supreme political power and authority of the nation-state. In the
economic field, the United States over the past fifty years has
entered into hundreds if not thousands of such sovereignty-
limiting bilateral and multilateral agreements on trade, investment, and other commercial activities. Of even greater consequence for constraining the sovereign right of action are security
alliances, such as within NATO and with South Korea, whereby
the United States is committed to go to war if foreign borders are
violated, and which include the presence of large numbers of

American troops along those borders as a trip wire to ensure that the United States honors its commitment to military engagement. The issue for all of these agreements is whether the benefits to the United States are worth the limitations they place on U.S. freedom of action, and it is in this context that the Uruguay Round agreement and NAFTA should be judged.

The WTO debate has rightly focused on the new and greatly strengthened dispute settlement mechanism. The new mechanism provides for reasonably prompt and reliable resolution of disputes about implementation of WTO commitments by a dispute panel, subject to an appellate review procedure. The United States, in fact, had pressed for more than twenty years for such a strengthened dispute procedure because other countries, with less open legal and judicial systems than prevail in the United States, were less apt to maintain market-opening GATT—and now WTO—commitments. The essential fact is that the dispute settlement procedure is limited to adjudication of the implementation of commitments already freely undertaken, such as to reduce a specified trade barrier or to provide foreign suppliers equal treatment with domestic companies under certain conditions. Moreover, even when the United States is found in violation of such a commitment, the follow-on action is not rigidly prescribed. The guilty party can either rectify implementation of the commitment, offer compensation through improved market access elsewhere, or ignore the panel finding and face retaliation through reduced access to the aggrieved party's market. Such third party arbitration for implementation of existing commitments is not unreasonable or unusual, and the United States stands to gain far more than it loses (if, in fact, having to comply with an existing agreement is considered a loss).

Similarly, NAFTA opened the Mexican market to U.S. exports and investment far more than it did for Mexican exports and investment in the United States. Mexican border restrictions were much higher than those in the United States, and new Mexican commitments in the areas of investment, protection of intellectual property, government procurement, financial services, and transportation were, for the most part, only providing what already existed in the far more open U.S. market. Moreover, preferential free access to the Mexican market compared with European and Asian exports to Mexico provides U.S. exporters a major advantage that is already evident in the growing U.S. market share for imports in Mexico. The NAFTA dispute settlement mechanism for antidumping and countervailing duty measures provides for a prompt determination of the proper application of existing laws by a binational panel, similar in concept to the new WTO procedure. In sum, the United States took on relatively few sovereignty-limiting new commitments in NAFTA while obtaining, in return, vastly improved preferential access to the Mexican market.

Limitations on the Effective Exercise of Sovereignty

Of greater consequence for U.S. sovereignty than the legal provisions of recent trade agreements are the effective limitations on the exercise of sovereign powers from the process of economic globalization itself. The most obvious example is the limitation imposed on national monetary policies by the globalization of financial markets and the private banking sector. Attempts by national monetary authorities to pursue policies contrary to international market forces are no longer sustainable and can lead to especially disruptive market reactions when they fail. Longstanding practices in developing countries of controlling monetary growth and interest rates in isolation from international capital markets are no longer feasible as emerging market economies rely on internal and external private capital that can seek more attractive alternatives on a global scale. The Mexican financial crisis of 1995 and the Thailand crisis of 1997 were examples of monetary authorities trying to control inflation and lower interest rates through an overvalued exchange rate, and then being overwhelmed by private market reactions. U.S. monetary policy is likewise increasingly constrained by its impact on the balance-of-payments and the global economy. The very high U.S. interest rates of the early 1980s contributed to domestic and global recessions and caused a sharp rise in the dollar, leading to a massive deterioration of the trade account—reactions that would be even stronger with the more integrated capital markets of the late 1990s.

The effective exercise of national economic sovereignty in other areas of policy is similarly curtailed, although the process is less obvious and less advanced than in the monetary field. Private investment decisions are influenced by national tax, labor, welfare, environmental, and other regulatory policies, and decisions about investment location are increasingly international in scope. Developing countries compete for foreign investment through tax and other incentives. Differences in labor and other social policies among EU members are leading to shifts in production and jobs both inside and outside the Union. The higher risks and costs of lawsuits against companies within the U.S. judicial system is a significant disincentive for new investment in some sectors in the United States by American and foreign companies.

These international constraints on national economic and social policies have always existed, but they are becoming more constraining as companies become more international in their decision-making, particularly about the location of production and jobs. The degree of such global corporate decision-making varies greatly by country, sector, and firm. Most U.S. firms remain primarily American in their organizational structure and good U.S. corporate citizens in their behavior related to U.S. foreign policy, but the direction of change is clearly toward more and more global orientation as increasing numbers of firms derive the majority of their sales and income from outside the United States. Just how global American corporate decision-making has become and how fast it is moving toward further globalization are central questions for understanding what is happening in the world economy, including the increasing limitations being placed on the practical exercise of sovereign economic powers.

Economic Dependence and National Security: The Sectoral Dimension

Growing dependence on foreign supplies and markets includes an inherent national security dimension in that nations can curtail or threaten to curtail economic relationships to coerce political actions by adversary economic partners, or simply to weaken their economic power, including defense production capability. Such national-security-related economic relationships vary widely in content by sector and country. The focus here is on the United States, starting with a sectoral assessment and then moving to country relationships.

The United States is among the most economically self-sufficient nations in the world, and, with the post–Cold War decline in Russian production capability, clearly the most self-sufficient in military production and new weapons development. U.S. imports are widely dispersed by sector, with heavy concentration in consumer goods and tropical food products, which have a relatively low potential for economic coercion by foreign suppliers. There are, however, two narrowly based exceptions to this generally low vulnerability situation—imports of oil and high technology military components—and one more broad-based concern about technology-intensive industries in general.

The import share of U.S. oil consumption was more than 50 percent in 1996, creating the potential for a disruptive impact, on the transportation sector in particular, if foreign supplies are curtailed. Technological advance should reduce this import dependency over time through higher domestic oil and oil-substitute energy production and more efficient consumption, but over the short- to medium-term the import vulnerability will continue and probably increase. This calls for an updated assessment of the degree of oil import vulnerability, in qualitative as well as quantitative terms, and including remedial policies.[26]

Reliance on imported components for military weapons systems is the other specific national security concern, but such concern appears to be declining compared with the late 1980s when Japan, in particular, was reaching parity with or surpassing the United States in certain advanced-technology sectors, and when one member of the Japanese Diet spoke of possibly withholding critical military components from the United States as commercial bargaining leverage. In any event, U.S. weapons procurement provides preference to a large extent for domestic suppliers, and new weapons development by U.S. firms is funded by the Department of Defense.

The more broad-based concern is that vertical integration across borders in certain technology-intensive U.S. industry sectors could threaten the overall strength of the U.S. economy if overseas supplies of key components were threatened by foreign government actions. Again, the concern was more keenly felt in the 1980s, particularly related to Japanese gains in the semiconducter sector, and has declined as U.S. production in this and other technology-intensive sectors has strengthened and become more competitive internationally. Such underlying vulnerability to foreign government actions nevertheless goes to the core of the economic globalization process and will inevitability grow as globalization continues.

Economic Dependence and National Security: The Trade Partner Dimension

The vulnerability of national security interests to economic dependence on foreign suppliers depends not only on the products involved, but also on the political reliability and diversity of foreign suppliers. The United States is far less likely to face a politically motivated cutback in oil supplies from Canada and Norway than from Iran and Iraq, and the more geographically dispersed oil supplies are, the less likely the chance of major curtailment in supply.

Apart from heavy dependence on Middle East oil, the United States has a highly diverse set of economic partnerships. Overall, trade breaks down to roughly 30 percent with East Asia, 30 percent with North America, 30 percent with Europe and smaller shares elsewhere. Moreover, two-thirds of total imports come from the industrialized democracies where political relationships are most positive and secure. Relations in the Western Hemisphere are also based on shared political values of democratic government and respect for individual rights, reinforced by growth-enhancing economic reforms, including free trade, all conducive to positive and secure trade relationships.

The more troubled U.S. foreign policy relationships, with one prominent exception, tend to be with countries of relatively small economic significance. Very poor, politically unstable countries and those racked by internal ethnic and tribal strife are at the periphery of the economic globalization process. The so-called rogue states that pose international security threats are likewise generally minor players in economic terms. Iran, Iraq, and Libya together, for example, supply only about 10 percent of world petroleum exports, which equates to a fraction of 1 percent of world merchandise exports.

The prominent exception is China, the one major U.S. economic partner with a troubled political/security relationship. Even in this case, however, while bilateral trade and investment are growing rapidly, U.S. imports from China remain concentrated in textiles and apparel, footwear, toys, sporting goods, and consumer electronics, not sectors of strategic importance. Over the longer-term, however, the U.S.-China economic relationship will likely become more deeply linked in structural terms, with concomitant deeper dependencies of a political/security character as well. This already important bilateral relationship, in fact, will become more and more central to the outcome for the relation between economic globalization and U.S. national security interests, as addressed in the next two issues.

Before turning to these longer-term issues, however, one other dimension of economic relations and U.S. national security interest is noteworthy, namely, the reverse situation whereby the United States applies economic sanctions against other countries to achieve foreign policy objectives. The more frequent use of such economic sanctions by the United States in the post–Cold War period, multilaterally and unilaterally, is a subject of intense debate, and two observations are simply inserted here. First, economic sanctions of whatever kind have limited capability to impose political change on authoritarian governments, while the poorer segments of the sanctioned country population and the private sector in general suffer the most. Second, unilateral economic sanctions almost never achieve significant foreign policy results and can easily become counterproductive.

Economic Globalization and the Changing Structure of the Global Economy

This issue and the following one of globalization as a force for political change are longer-term in their impact, but not that much longer. Fundamental change in the structure of the global economy will take place over the next decade or two, and far more so over the coming fifty years. A half-century of Cold War, centered on a geostrategic, negative sum power struggle between two global military alliances is being followed by a new half-century based on a political-economic, positive sum change of an increasingly multilateral character. This new world order does not yet have a name, but a central defining force is economic globalization as described here. The outcome will have profound effect on U.S. national security and the effective exercise of sovereign powers.

The starting point for describing the changing structure of the global economy is the one-four-one configuration introduced earlier—one billion people in the advanced industrialized democracies; four billion in the emerging market economies of Asia, Latin America, and Central Europe; and one billion in the mostly very poor countries elsewhere. The middle grouping of four billion reaps the largest and fastest benefits from globalization, leading to a fundamental shift in orientation of global economic power. As noted earlier, developing countries have recently been growing at double the rate of the industrialized countries, and this difference is projected to continue at least through the end of the decade. These higher rates of economic growth, moreover, reflect in part higher rates of population growth in developing countries—2 percent compared with less than 1 percent in the industrialized countries. A number of European countries, including Germany, Italy, Russia, and Spain, already have or are projected to have a declining population in absolute terms.

What this means in twenty-five years, from 1995 to 2020, roughly projected (developing country GDP growth of 5 percent versus 2.5 percent growth for industrialized countries, on a ppp basis) is a decline in the share of global GDP held by industrialized countries from 54 percent to 39 percent, and for the United States from 21 percent to 15 percent. The share of global population in industrialized countries, based on UN projections, will likewise decline from 16 percent to 12 percent, and in the United States from 5 percent to 4 percent. These projections are very crude, but if the current economic globalization process continues in anything like its current form, the direction of change is clear, and the declines projected for the United States and other industrialized countries are feasible and, if anything, conservative.

From the perspective of U.S. sovereign freedom of action and national security, such projections can be disturbing. Indeed, they should be unless this economic change is accompanied by political change toward greater cooperation, trust, and shared values among the existing and emerging economic powers. Looking ahead, a central question for U.S. foreign policy can indeed be formulated: How can the U.S. manage international economic relations, not only to its own commercial advantage but in a way so as to maximize desirable change in the world political order as well?

Economic Globalization as a Force for Political Change

Surprisingly, seven years after the dissolution of the Soviet Union, there is little agreement among U.S. political leaders and experts about the content of the new set of international relationships. Nondescript terms such as "new world order" and "post–Cold War world" are indicative of the conceptual vacuum. Three competing lines of thought are that the international community of nations is entering an era of either neo-geopolitics, dangerous cultural clashes, or unprecedented cooperation based on the triumph of liberal democracy and economic liberalism.

The new situation, in fact, has elements of all three paradigms, and their relative roles will be determined to a decisive extent by the course of economic globalization and how it is managed by the governments of the major economic powers. The globalization process is driven largely by technological change and the initiative of increasingly multinational private enterprises, but the response of governments will also be critical, particularly for moving the process toward the clearly preferred third paradigm of a world composed principally of market-oriented democracies, working together to contain common threats such as the proliferation of weapons of mass destruction and terrorism and to respond to global environmental and other problems. This policy response will center on trade, investment, and a broadening array of related economic policies, which is the substance of the succeeding five essays. The underlying policy question addressed here first, however, is whether economic globalization, managed in the direction of more open national markets, can be expected, in the process, to change political behavior as well, and in the direction of more democratic governments and more cooperative relationships among them. Are new geopolitical rivalries and major cultural clashes inevitable, or is the world entering at least a new, more benign phase if not the end of history? The course of the four billion people in the emerging market economies, in particular, is central to change in the world economy, but how will their political and cultural orientations evolve, and what should the United States do to influence the outcome?

These are questions of vital importance to U.S. foreign policy formulation which deserve a more deeply engaged, analytic response from officials and experts, cutting across political, economic, and cultural lines. To help stimulate the debate, a few concluding comments are offered in support of the feasibility of the third paradigm.

Growing evidence indeed exists that economic modernization and growth produce a political constituency more disposed toward and insistent upon democratic government. An enlarged, educated middle class, devolution of power away from the central government, and the reduction of public corruption through economic deregulation, including trade liberalization, are contributing factors. The results are evident in Central Europe, Latin America, and parts of Asia (most remarkably in South Korea and Taiwan). Another pervasive contributing factor to the course of economic and political change is the explosive growth in the availability of information, free or at minimal cost, which is the distinctive hallmark of the current wave of economic globalization. Though exceedingly difficult to factor into the overall equation for change, this element is the most frequently cited. Perhaps information should be considered a distinct factor of production, a challenge for model-building economists. In any event, "information age" should be part of the answer to the post–Cold War nomenclature question.

Specifying more precisely how and to what extent political behavior is changing as a result of economic globalization is even more speculative, but change is taking place, and all indications are that it is broadly in the direction of a more rational, scientifically based response to mutual problems, with a growing optimistic sense, at least among the more educated strata of societies, that progress is obtainable. It is a resurgence, in effect, of the extraordinarily creative thinking of the eighteenth century Age of Reason in Europe and the United States, only now on a more global scale.[27] After a nineteenth century debilitated by nationalist rivalries and a twentieth century devastated by two hot and one cold world wars, the twenty-first century could emerge a new information age of reason, driven largely by economic globalization as a force for political as well as economic change. At a minimum, a "new information age of reason" should be the normative goal for U.S. foreign policy, while providing a contingent response to the post–Cold War nomenclature question.

A Net Assessment

This presentation of economic globalization has thus far served two purposes. First, it provided a practical framework for discussing the many interrelated aspects of the subject in a complete and systematic manner. To this end, the organization of subject headings moved from a broad definition of globalization to a more detailed description of its dimensions to the three main categories of impact on U.S. interests.

Second, the presentation aided the reader in developing a better sense of priorities as to what the important policy-relevant issues are, and assessing the degree of knowledge and understanding currently available about them. Given the highly complex and dynamic context of current economic globalization, there is no question that such knowledge is far less than complete, and in some areas it is sketchy at best. The following specific issues and related gaps in understanding should be priorities for further analytic work:

Clearer understanding is needed as to whether and to what extent the current "third wave" of economic globalization is indeed distinct—a discontinuity—from what has gone before. The case presented here holds that the current wave is very distinct, with far-reaching implications, but this assessment is not shared by all or perhaps even the majority of observers. A closely related issue concerns the economic "gains from trade" from globalization writ large, including FDI, nonequity affiliations, and other cross-border economic activities, and which, in turn, is related to a more accurate assessment of economic growth and productivity trends in the U.S. economy. Professional economists have divergent opinions on these issues which are central to assessing the impact of globalization on U.S. interests. Although the highlighted guiding principle that it is more important to be roughly right than precisely wrong is well understood by a new breed of international entrepreneurs organizing high risk—and even higher potential profit—investment projects in emerging market economies, it can be alien culture for articles appearing in professional economic journals.

Better understanding of the motivations and activities of multinational corporations, a moving target for investigators, is also central to the globalization process. The catalytic role of financial and telecommunications services would benefit especially from more in-depth analysis. The full dynamic gains from trade and investment in these sectors, both for the providers and purchasers of such services, are far greater than reflected in available data on trade and FDI, and better means to assess them would be most enlightening. More generally, greater attention to the microbehavior of companies, operating across borders and within national economies, as they reorient toward "the management of innovation," would provide critical insight to the current process of economic globalization.

Finally, the relation between economic globalization and U.S. foreign policy objectives, although treated here in highly summary form, should be the most important area for national debate. Inhibiting this debate is the compartmentalization of discussion between the political/security and political/economic groupings involved in formulating and implementing U.S. foreign policy. The former, populated largely by "Cold War warriors" and geostrategic thinkers, tends to equate foreign policy with conflict-related national security interests, which propels Bosnia, Haiti, Somalia, and the UN Security Council to the top of the agenda for U.S. foreign policy. The latter, political/ economic grouping consists of economists, technocrats, and private sector leaders who see U.S. foreign policy more in economic terms as presented here. The two groupings live and operate in largely separate worlds, with the political/security contingent still dominant within U.S. foreign policy councils.

Given all of the foregoing limitations on knowledge and understanding, the third purpose of this essay is to make a best possible net assessment of economic globalization and the U.S. interest, and to relate it to current U.S. policies in support of an increasingly more open if not free trade international economic system—in other words, strong policy reinforcement of the globalization process. The assessment is as follows:

1. The economic globalization process since the mid-1980s is unprecedented in its geographic scope and impact on national economies, a process projected to continue if not accelerate indefinitely. It is driven by the dramatic triumph of economic liberalism in government policies throughout the world, rapid technological change, and the growing internationalization of private enterprise. The globalization genie is out of the bottle short of some unforseen major international catastrophe.

2. The economic gains from this sustained growth in international trade, investment, and other cross-border economic activities are substantial, probably on the order of 1 percent or more of incremental annual growth for the U.S. economy, and considerably greater for the emerging market economies in Asia, Latin America, and Central Europe. These economic gains are larger than generally recognized, mainly because the dynamic gains from new investment, new technology application, and corporate restructuring resulting from more open trade and greater international competition are impossible to measure fully. They have also been difficult to assimilate conceptually with a U.S. economy long believed to be suffering low productivity growth, but this mind-set is belatedly changing as the recalculated, higher U.S. growth experience gains wider acceptance.

3. The adjustment impact of globalization on the U.S. economy, in contrast, is less of a problem than widely perceived. Protectionists and other interest groups opposed to a liberal trade policy have greatly exaggerated the extent of negative impact on labor in particular. In fact, the globalization process creates jobs comparable in number to those displaced, and the new jobs tend to be more productive and higher-paying. Job displacement from globalization in any event is a very small share of total job changes within the U.S. economy and should be addressed through broader policies for worker retraining and strengthening of the education system. A significant adjustment problem for the U.S. economy, however, concerns the persistent large current account deficit and consequent foreign debt buildup since the early 1980s. Rectifying this debt calls for fiscal policies to increase domestic savings and a serious reappraisal of the longstanding dollar-based international financial system in the new circumstances of third wave economic globalization.

4. An assessment of economic globalization and national sovereignty/security needs to distinguish the short- to medium-term (5–10 years) from the longer-term outlook. For the short- to medium-term, negative consequences for national security are minimal except for the potentially disruptive impact of a curtailment of oil imports from the Middle East. Overall, the United States remains highly self-sufficient in technology-intensive industries, including defense-related production. Trading partners are geographically diverse and imports, predominantly from countries that are politically stable and friendly, are mostly consumer goods and other products not sensitive to national security relationships. The exercise of national sovereignty over monetary and related economic policies is increasingly constrained by the internationalization of financial markets, but this constraint is principally a discipline on sound policies at the national level, and there is no apparent major threat to the U.S. banking system from such financial globalization.

5. The longer-term impact (20–50 years) of economic globalization on U.S. national sovereignty/security is of far greater consequence and uncertainty. The relative economic power position of the United States—and the current grouping of industrialized democracies—will decline substantially, and the capability of potential adversaries to exploit economic interdependencies and modernize military capabilities will increase correspondingly. U.S. foreign policy objectives need to be redirected to meet this inevitable political/economic/security challenge. The central objective should be to broaden the community of industrialized democracies as economic modernization—and globalization—continue, to the point where it comprises the large majority of world population as well as economic and military power, with the four billion people in the emerging market economies the critical mass. A favorable response is by no means assured—history in ideological terms has not yet ended—and actions by industrialized democracy governments, and by the U.S. government most of all, will play a critical role. The current path of economic globalization presents the technical parameters for a new information age of reason, but inspired public and private sector leadership will ultimately determine the outcome.

What the U.S. policy response to economic globalization should be, based on this net assessment, is wide-ranging in scope, pervading virtually all aspects of national life. The front and most direct line of response, however, will continue to be in the areas of international trade, investment, and a broadening set of trade-related, mostly regulatory policies. The basic policy alternatives, expressed most succinctly, are to rollback, hunker down, or take the bull by the horns.

A rollback of the liberal—and increasingly free trade—policies of the past half-century would have a substantial adverse effect on the U.S. economy and would undermine any U.S. leadership role in shaping the broader world economic and political order. Moreover, it would have only limited impact on slowing down the course of economic globalization throughout the rest of the world. Presidential candidate Pat Buchanan was at least straight forward in his rollback position—pull out of the WTO, cancel NAFTA, and impose across-the-board high tariffs on imports from low-wage developing countries—but very few Americans rallied in support of this neo-Luddite approach.

The second, hunker down alternative entails maintaining existing trade agreements while halting additional regional free trade and other ambitious trade liberalizing proposals for the indefinite future. This can have appeal in view of the extraordinary course of economic globalization over the past ten years and the great uncertainty as to where it is heading. The complex interaction of various regional and functional initiatives currently being considered in the absence of any comprehensive economic strategy for the longer term constitutes good cause to sit back and take stock. The problem with this approach, again, is that the globalization process and the actions of other governments would continue while the United States abdicates its longstanding central role to influence the course of events. The lack of U.S. support for a broad-based WTO plan of action over the next several years would stultify the fledgling multilateral trade forum, shifting interest even more to regional initiatives. The

Europeans would continue to broaden and deepen their regional free trade grouping, East Asians would be drawn closer together in the absence of the APEC free trade objective, and South Americans would consolidate around Brazil/Mercosur if the United States ceased its active pursuit of a Free Trade Agreement of the Americas (FTAA). Economic globalization would continue, but with the United States in a passive role and the policy initiative shifted to other regions. There is considerable support in the United States for such a trade strategy.

The third, "take the bull by the horns" policy alternative is favored by majorities within both major political parties in the United States. The central objective is to continue the market-opening course, on a mutual basis with trading partners, and in effect to provide further policy reinforcement to the economic globalization process. The specific goals and modalities for pursuing this course, however, are matters of great controversy. What should the United States be seeking at the multilateral WTO, regional free trade, and bilateral negotiating levels, including priority sector and functional objectives at each level? The complex prospect for moving this liberal trade policy agenda forward over the coming five to ten years is the subject of the following five essays. What this first, introductory essay has tried to demonstrate is that the substantive and conceptual underpinnings for a liberal trade policy—and for the real prospect of going from here to free trade—have changed greatly over the past ten years and will continue to change in the period ahead. Economic globalization is at the center of this dynamic process of change, and the very graphic American term, "taking the bull by the horns," is a fitting analogy for the trade policy challenge ahead.

2

The Post–Uruguay Round
Free Trade Debate

A debate about free trade is under way in the United States, but it is not fully engaged and is ill-defined in conceptual terms, including what free trade means today. There is no question, however, that the debate marks a fundamental shift in orientation for international trade relationships. For almost fifty years, the multilateral trading system, centered on the GATT, involved a process of gradual trade liberalization among all members. Free trade—the complete elimination of border restrictions—however, was never seriously pursued or considered feasible, even as a long-term objective. Now, in contrast, a metamorphosis is taking place in trade relationships—free trade has become an explicit objective, on a multilateral as well as regional basis.

One problem with understanding this metamorphosis in trade relationships is that it is caught up in a broader trade policy debate conducted in more traditional terms between liberal traders and protectionists. The NAFTA and Uruguay Round agreements, approved by the U.S. Congress in 1993 and 1994, were major steps toward more open markets, and several post–Uruguay Round initiatives, as explained below, lead further in that direction. On the other side of this broader debate is a growing array of voices and forces arguing to restrict trade. Political figures, including Democratic house minority leader Richard Gephardt (D-Mo.), Republican presidential candidate Patrick Buchanan, and Ross Perot, decry the loss of U.S. jobs resulting from NAFTA and the Uruguay Round. Other leading politicians are raising serious concerns about national sovereignty and liberal trade agreements. The first Clinton administration pursued a limited agenda in the newly created WTO, while protectionist interests turn to means other than tariffs, such as antidumping complaints, to limit foreign competition. Pessimism runs especially strong among free trade economists, who see the liberal trading system, laboriously created since World War II, under severe threat. A noteworthy example of such anguish is the 1995 book *American Trade Policy: A Tragedy in the Making* by Anne Krueger, then president-elect of the American Economic Association. Krueger explains "the tragedy of current U.S. trade policy," which has been "increasingly schizophrenic." She concludes that although the open multilateral trading system has served the world well, the United States has failed to exert leadership in support of it.[1] Many of her conclusions are well taken, but her analysis should have probed deeper into fundamental changes taking place in trade relationships.

The conclusion drawn here is that the liberal trade momentum of recent years will prevail, perhaps even intensify. The rationale for such a conclusion goes beyond reading the short-term political tea leaves and rests largely on the underlying dynamic forces of free trade. The principal purpose of this essay, in fact, is to disentangle the evolving free trade relationships from the broader trade policy debate, with particular emphasis on political and economic implications for the structure of the world trading system. The essay begins with an assessment of the free trade process now under way defined in terms of three interacting dimensions: multilateral free trade by sector; comprehensive regional free trade; and the broadening scope of policies included in free trade relationships. Commentary on two primary driving forces for free trade, namely, the rapidly expanding "dynamic gains from trade" and the private sector leadership role, follows, and, finally, a presentation of a multilateral/regional free trade synthesis brings together the various components of the debate in terms of what the future course of trade relationships could or should be.

The Three Dimensions of Free Trade

Free trade can be pursued unilaterally, as was done by Hong Kong, simply by eliminating import barriers to all trading partners on a nondiscriminatory or most-favored-nation (MFN) basis. Free trade areas are also permitted under Article XXIV of the GATT, whereby barriers are eliminated on substantially all of the trade among a self-selected group of countries while tariffs remain for imports from nonmembers. If a common external tariff is formed for nonmembers, such a free trade area is called a customs union. Until the mid-1980s, relatively little trade, except raw materials and some agricultural commodities, was duty-free on an MFN basis, and regional free trade was limited principally to Western Europe. By the mid-1990s, however, free trade on both an MFN and regional basis had grown substantially and further important steps are under active discussion. This free trade process involves three dimensions: multilateral free trade by sector; regional free trade agreements; and a broadening scope of policy commitments.

Multilateral Free Trade by Sector

The prolonged Uruguay Round negotiations of 1986–93 initially paid little attention to tariff reductions and later bogged down in attempts to create a formula for doing so. Only in 1990, at the initiative of private sector leaders in the United States and other industrialized countries, was the approach of "zero-for-zero" tariff elimination by sector pursued, beginning with the pharmaceutical sector and later extending to eight other sectors, including farm machinery, medical equipment, furniture, and toys. The final Uruguay Round agreement, as a consequence, resulted in more than doubling—from 20 percent to 44 percent—the share of nonagricultural imports by industrialized countries that will be free of duties on an MFN basis.

In 1995, the "Quad" countries (the United States, the European Union [EU], Japan, and Canada) launched a post–Uruguay Round initiative to eliminate remaining tariffs in the information technology sector—computers, semiconductors, telecommunications equipment and software—and to align other technology-related policies as part of a broader global information infrastructure strategy. At the November 1996 WTO ministerial meeting in Singapore, agreement was reached to eliminate such duties by the year 2000. As a result, the share of nonagricultural imports by these countries that are duty-free on an MFN basis will increase further, to about 50 percent.

The WTO has a mandate to develop additional sectoral free trade agreements and would be wise to do so. The chemical sector, for example, emerged from the Uruguay Round with industrialized country tariffs harmonized mostly at a low 5 percent level, and the final move to zero would not be difficult. The automotive sector—troubled by nontariff barriers in the Japanese market and EU quotas on imports from Japan—has generally low levels of tariffs, which could be phased out in the context of a broader agreement on nontariff barriers to market access.[2]

This path of MFN tariff elimination by sector, however, faces two major problems in the WTO that will limit the outcome. The first is that the sectors adopted for free trade are those in which multinational companies tend to dominate as they seek to benefit from market rationalization on a global scale. Other sectors, including textiles, footwear, and most of agriculture, remain highly protected with little inclination toward free trade on the part of the industrialized countries. The net result is thus likely to be a very uneven structure of tariffs by sector.

The second problem is that sectoral free trade up to this point is not fully multilateral, but limited, for the most part, to the industrialized grouping. Developing countries played a more active role in the Uruguay Round but did not participate in tariff elimination by sector, and the more advanced developing countries in Asia and Latin America continue to maintain relatively high tariffs. The pharmaceutical and other industries supporting multilateral free trade were disappointed over the lack of participation by developing countries in the Uruguay Round, and they continue to complain about the "free ride"—free access to industrialized country markets while maintaining high protection at home—afforded to such countries. The Singapore information technology agreement included partial participation by some developing countries, but even in this sector where developing countries have much to gain and relatively few vested interests, participation remains limited. The continuing asymmetry in market access will thus create a problem for any future round of multilateral trade liberalization in the WTO.

Comprehensive Regional Free Trade

The most active dimension of the free trade debate thus far concerns the proliferation of regional free trade agreements since the mid-1980s, which was triggered by the reversal of long-standing U.S. policy opposing such agreements. The United States first negotiated free trade agreements with Israel, Canada, and Mexico through NAFTA. Then, in 1994, agreement was reached to negotiate free trade in the Western Hemisphere by 2005 (beginning with Chile and an interim "NAFTA-parity" agreement with the Caribbean Basin countries) and then in the Asia-Pacific region by 2020, with a 2010 date for the more advanced Asia-Pacific countries, including the United States and Japan.

The EU, meanwhile, has been broadening its regional free trade grouping in the wake of the collapse of the Soviet bloc. Austria, Finland, and Sweden joined in 1994; interim free trade agreements leading to membership have been implemented with the Czech Republic, Hungary, Poland, and Slovakia; and a customs union agreement with Turkey is well advanced. Further free trade agreements are under negotiation or agreed to in principle with about 15 additional countries in Eastern Europe and the Mediterranean Basin. Elsewhere in the world, subregional free trade agreements include Australia/New Zealand, the Association of Southeast Asian Nations or ASEAN (Brunei, Indonesia, Malaysia, Myanmar, the Philippines, Singapore, Thailand, and Vietnam), and the Southern Cone Common Market or Mercosur (Argentina, Brazil, Paraguay, and Uruguay).

Another possible free trade agreement, with far-reaching political as well as economic implications, is a transatlantic free trade agreement (TAFTA), reflecting the dynamic interaction among the various regional free trade initiatives. U.S. free trade objectives in the Western Hemisphere and the Asia-Pacific region have left the transatlantic relationship, long the backbone of U.S. economic and security relationships, in a subsidiary position—the dog that isn't barking. Some Europeans are concerned that they may be left out of a dominant economic grouping that embraces the Western Hemisphere and the Asia-Pacific. Indeed, initial proponents of some kind of EU/NAFTA accord were Europeans, plus Canadian prime minister Jean Chrétien. The first Clinton administration reaction was cool to adverse to the idea, although some influential Americans with a more strategic perspective of the world economy, including House Speaker Newt Gingrich (R-Ga.) and former secretary of state Henry Kissinger, advocate a TAFTA.[3]

The growing relative importance of regional free trade agreements is apparent in the share of world exports included in them. Trade within the EU and NAFTA alone accounts for almost 40 percent of world exports. EU agreements with the Central European countries and Turkey, Australia/New Zealand, ASEAN, and Mercosur raise this figure by another 4 to 5 percent. The further inclusion of Western Hemisphere and APEC free trade agreements would increase the share to 65 percent, and inclusion of a TAFTA pushes the share to over 70 percent. In terms of trade coverage, regional free trade agreements are clearly headed toward a majority position within the overall trading system.

Two noteworthy aspects of the regional trend make such free trade agreements the leading edge for the evolution of the trading system in broader terms. First, they are able to bridge the dichotomy between industrialized and developing countries that has existed in the GATT and been carried over into the WTO under the rubric of "special and differential treatment."[4] In the multilateral system, developing countries are not expected to provide fully reciprocal access to their markets, which has been a continuing cause of friction, as noted above with respect to tariff elimination by sector in the Uruguay Round. Regional free trade agreements, in contrast, tend not to make this distinction. Within NAFTA, Mexico is eliminating virtually all border restrictions, in agriculture as well as in industry, from the more than 70 percent of its imports coming from the United States and Canada, while in the Uruguay Round, Mexico maintained MFN tariffs in the 10 to 20 percent range and only agreed to bind many of them against future increase at 40 percent. Extension of NAFTA to Chile and others in the Western Hemisphere should follow the same pattern—little or no special and differential treatment. Similarly, EU membership agreements, earlier with Greece and Portugal and now with the Central European countries, are based on the principle of fully reciprocal elimination of import restrictions, even though all of these countries can be considered to some extent less developed.[5]

The second aspect placing regional free trade agreements on the leading edge of the trading system evolution involves integration or harmonization of other trade-related policies. This broadening scope of policies encompassed by free trade agreements is, in fact, the third and least clearly defined dimension of the free trade debate.

The Broadening Scope of Policy Coverage

The definition of free trade can be limited to the elimination of border restrictions on imports—tariffs and quotas—leaving all other related economic policies unchanged. GATT Article XXIV is so drafted for regional free trade agreements, and tariff elimination by sector in the Uruguay Round was negotiated on this basis. Trade agreements over time, however, have tended to include a broader and broader scope of other trade-related policies. This trend is a reflection, in part, of the fact that as border restrictions are reduced or eliminated, other policies become relatively more important in influencing trade flows and thus need to be assimilated in the trade relationship. Even more important, the structure of world trade and investment has changed greatly (particularly since about 1980, as explained in essay 1), creating pressures for a far broader scope of policy response.

The broadening scope of policy inclusion in the international trading system has been proceeding on various fronts, through multilateral as well as regional agreements. The multilateral Uruguay Round agreement broadened the mandate of the GATT/WTO to include trade in services, which by definition extended coverage to investment policy for companies delivering services abroad. The Uruguay Round also added the protection of intellectual property rights to the multilateral trading system, as well as expanded coverage of technical standards and certain trade-related investment measures. Finally, the agreement called for further consideration of competition and investment policies in the future, now being done by WTO working groups, and a multilateral investment agreement is already being negotiated in the Organization for Economic Cooperation and Development (OECD), presumably for later incorporation into the WTO.

The broadening policy scope of trade relationships is most prominent, however, in regional free trade agreements, principally the EU and NAFTA, which constitute the leading edge for the trend toward deeper policy integration. The EU has established the goals of a single integrated market and monetary union, while NAFTA has a more modest but still comprehensive scope of policy coverage, including investment policy, protection of intellectual property rights, financial services, transportation, and side agreements for labor and environmental standards.

Free trade, therefore, has two limiting definitions: at a minimum the elimination of border restrictions and nothing more, and at a maximum full economic and monetary union more or less as being pursued by the EU (and as exists among states within the United States). Other free trade agreements, including NAFTA, fall somewhere in between, and where the lines are drawn is based on political as well as economic factors. Why, for example, a monetary union for the EU and not for NAFTA? The reality of deepening economic interdependencies, in any event, increases the relative economic benefits of broader policy integration, and this is most apparent within what are appropriately termed "comprehensive" free trade agreements.

Regional free trade agreements can also create the conditions for dealing with problems in policy areas that cannot be addressed adequately within the multilateral trade system. Antidumping procedures, for example, which are subject to growing protectionist abuse throughout the world, can more easily be eliminated inside free trade groupings, as they have been in the EU, provided that antitrust and other elements of competition policy in member states are made reasonably comparable. This step would indeed be highly desirable for NAFTA.[6]

Finally, the broadening scope of trade-related policy integration—and thus the broadening definition of free trade—is being driven as much by market forces as by government design, which is fundamental to understanding where the international trading system is heading over both the short and longer term. These market forces, in turn, can be assessed in terms of two interacting components: the rapidly expanding dynamic gains from trade (described in detail in essay 1) and the private sector leadership role.

The Private Sector Leadership Role

The movement toward free trade, by region and by sector, has resulted in part from the initiative of governments and in part from private sector leadership. President Ronald Reagan had a vision of free trade within North America that he pursued with characteristic tenacity, and the surprise decision of Mexican President Carlos Salinas de Gortari in 1990 to seek a free trade agreement with the United States was critical for NAFTA. Key European political leaders, likewise, were dedicated to the formation of a united Europe in the early postwar years and their successors are now deeply engaged in broadening and deepening the EU. Private sector leaders, however, have also come to play a more active role in developing new market-opening initiatives, most prominently in the United States, but with a growing habit of collaboration among North Americans, Europeans, and Japanese. In recent years, determined private sector leaders have often been out in front of hesitant governments.

Private sectors are, of course, not monolithic when it comes to trade policy. The protectionist interests of some firms compete with the liberal trade objectives of others. Nevertheless, the strong and growing tendency among the majority of private sector leaders is not only for continued trade liberalization, but for definitive moves to free trade on a pragmatic, step-by-step basis. This tendency in corporate policy orientation derives from the globalization of markets. Large investments of international market scope, with major trade components, require security of market access, the flexibility to adjust production as markets evolve, and a minimum degree of bureaucratic and administrative interference by governments. Free trade at the border and reasonable comparability in other trade- and investment-related policies constitute the best policy framework for multinational business.

A more assertive private sector role in establishing liberal and free trade policy objectives can be traced to the late 1970s, when the U.S. private sector insisted that trade in services be brought within the GATT multilateral trading system. Pressures were brought on a less committed executive branch through Congress. The U.S. private sector then joined with its European counterparts to press their case with even more reluctant European governments, and the service sector became a primary negotiating objective of the Uruguay Round. Similarly, the U.S. and other industrialized governments were undecided whether to pursue the protection of intellectual property rights in the Uruguay Round. The decisive move came from the U.S. private sector in late 1985, shortly before the Uruguay Round agenda was adopted, first to convince the U.S. government to pursue such an objective as a high priority, and then, together with European and Japanese business organizations, to draw up a statement of specific negotiating objectives that became the industrialized country mandate for the Round.

Tariff elimination by sector in the Uruguay Round, as noted earlier, was largely a private sector initiative as well. Most governments were seeking some formula for across-the-board percentage cuts in tariffs, with little success, when private sector deliberations came up with the simpler concept of sectoral free trade, whereby all companies would end up competing on an equal basis with minimal government interference. The 1995 initiative for free trade in the information technology sector is an even more interesting example of private sector initiative because European governments, in particular, insisted on maintaining high protection for the semiconductor industry up to the end of the Uruguay Round only two years earlier. European companies in the computer sector, however, understood that the resulting higher cost of semiconductors undermines their competitive position throughout this rapidly growing sector.

Comprehensive regional free trade has also been supported consistently by most of the private sector because it permits a broader geographic scope of market rationalization. U.S. private sector support for NAFTA was critical to its success, while European and Japanese firms were not openly opposed, in good part because they, too, can now invest and trade in an integrated North American market. The initiatives in 1994 to achieve free trade in the Western Hemisphere and the Asia-Pacific region also came about through strong and pointed support from private sector leaders in the face of initially disinterested or hesitant government attitudes in Washington and other capitals. Yet another case in which private sector leaders were out in front of governments is the OECD initiative for a multilateral agreement on investment, which the OECD private sector advisory committee had been advocating strongly for several years before governments finally responded. Looking ahead, the evolution of the concept of a TAFTA will also greatly, and perhaps critically, be influenced by deliberations that will likely take place among private sector leaders on both sides of the Atlantic, probably within the Transatlantic Business Dialogue established in 1995.

A Multilateral/Regional Synthesis

The foregoing outlines the principal elements of substance underlying the post–Uruguay Round free trade debate, which can be recapitulated as follows: Important trade relationships are moving toward free trade, within sectors and regions, to the point where free trade could soon be dominant in the overall trading system. At both the sectoral and regional levels, moreover, free trade is increasingly "comprehensive" in that agreements to eliminate trade barriers at the border are linked to commitments on other trade-related policies, principally in the areas of technology, investment, and competition policies. The overall process is being driven by the enormous and growing gains from trade, based largely on the application of new technologies. The net result is a transformation of international trade relationships writ large to include direct investment and technology transfer, with important political as well as economic implications.

The debate itself concerns the policy response to these rapidly evolving circumstances, and in particular a strategy for reconciling the momentum toward regional free trade with the reinvigorated but still relatively loosely drawn multilateral trading system contained in the newly created WTO. There are many facets to such a strategy, but unfortunately, as stated at the outset, the debate up to this point is not fully engaged and remains conceptually ill-defined. Some oppose further trade liberalization and would like to roll back the Uruguay Round and NAFTA agreements, but their argumentation is essentially episodic demagoguery, largely related to the short-term effects of the 1995 Mexican financial crisis, and little serious attention is given to the impact on U.S. interests of termination of these agreements. Private sector leaders, for the most part, support specific steps toward free trade on a case-by-case basis rather than in conceptual terms of where the overall trading system is headed. Many in the economics profession are predisposed to focus analysis on the limited static effects from free trade rather than on the full impact on world economic relationships. Some academic economists also tend to see multilateral trade liberalization and regional free trade agreements as "either/or" competitors, and hold a deep-seated preference for unambiguous, "first-best" multilateralism.[7]

The challenge of formulating a broad trade strategy at this important post–Cold War juncture is, in any event, one of international economic statesmanship, and it is in this context that the lack of a fully engaged debate—and leadership—is most disappointing. The strategic vision of post–World War II leaders, which created the Bretton Woods economic system, including the GATT, the West European economic union centered on Franco-German reconciliation, and the North Atlantic Treaty Organization security alliance against the Soviet threat, is nowhere to be found. "The vision thing," scorned by the Bush administration, has been largely excluded from a Clinton administration trade policy dedicated primarily to short-term negotiating objectives. In any event, from mid-1995 through 1996, trade policy for both major American political parties became largely a tactical matter related to the 1996 election campaign, a politically motivated schizophrenia to use Krueger's term. European leaders, meanwhile, were preoccupied with broadening their regional grouping without antagonizing farmers and other special interests, while Japan pursues its economic interests in consistently pragmatic rather than conceptual terms. The lack of interest in strategic thinking about the trading system was clearly apparent at recent economic summit meetings of the group of seven industrialized countries (G-7). At Naples in 1994, the United States proposed a new multilateral trade initiative, "Global 2000," but without being able to specify what it would consist of, and others understandably rejected it. At subsequent meetings in 1995, 1996, and 1997, trade strategy was simply not addressed beyond general support for the WTO.

The principal recommendation to be derived from this presentation is that a full-scale debate on short- and longer-term objectives for the international trading system writ large, including investment, competition, and technology-oriented policies, should be undertaken. In particular, these objectives should focus on synthesizing the largely separate multilateral and regional tracks of policy currently engaged and work toward a reasonably well-defined, integrated trade structure. The following four essays are designed to stimulate such debate, first by examining in greater detail the regional prospects for the United States across the Atlantic, the Pacific, and within the Western Hemisphere, and then by laying out three alternative strategies for achieving the multilateral/regional synthesis based on the comprehensive definition of free trade presented here.

3

Free Trade Across the Atlantic

Growing interest since 1994 in a Transatlantic Free Trade Agreement (TAFTA) reflects the dynamic among regional free trade groupings that is evolving within the international trading system. The EU is evolving to the east and NAFTA to the south in the Western Hemisphere and westward across the Pacific. Why not the transatlantic trade axis that has been at the center of the GATT trading system for fifty years? At a minimum, a TAFTA between the EU and NAFTA would head off the prospect of Europe and the Western Hemisphere drifting apart into adversarial economic blocs. In a positive sense, it could provide the bridging mechanism for reconciling the momentum toward comprehensive regional free trade and the multilateral WTO.

Beyond these obvious starting points, however, there has been only limited analysis of the specific issues involved in the creation of a TAFTA. The most comprehensive study of a new transatlantic trade initiative is *Transatlantic Trade: A Strategic Agenda,* by Ellen Frost, which contains valuable analysis of the motivations for such an initiative, but the study dismisses a TAFTA in a rather cursory manner and concentrates on a proposal for a less clearly defined, nondiscriminatory North Atlantic Economic Community, or NATEC.[1] This essay remains focused on a TAFTA initiative as a preferential free trade agreement in accordance with Article XXIV of the GATT and examines the economic and political rationale for such an initiative as well as initial steps for launching it. The rationale has three components—the substantive composition of a TAFTA, the impact on the overall international trading system, and the foreign policy consequences—which are addressed in turn, while the concluding section sketches out first steps that could be taken to lay the groundwork for opening formal negotiations.

The Substantive Composition

The substantive composition of a TAFTA would be relatively straight forward and far less daunting than, for example, free trade across the Pacific or even within the Western Hemisphere. Indeed, frustration over the lack of substantive progress toward the free trade goal within the APEC framework has produced a negative reaction toward any further "grand design" steps in international trade, including a TAFTA, but this is a misleading analogy. Moving the final steps to free trade across the Atlantic would be relatively easy, with the partial exception of agriculture addressed below. It bears no comparison with the obstacles to free trade between the United States and China within APEC, or even between the United States and Brazil in the Western Hemisphere.

The elimination of remaining nonagricultural tariffs would be the central commitment of a TAFTA, and in this respect, the North Atlantic nations are already most of the way there on a nondiscriminatory, MFN basis. As a result of the Uruguay Round agreement, the share of nonagricultural imports of industrialized countries entering duty-free will more than double from 20 percent to 44 percent. The post–Uruguay Round initiative to eliminate remaining duties in the information technology sector will bring this figure to about 50 percent. Other tariffs are generally low. There are a few peaks remaining in tariff structures, most notably for textiles and apparel, but transatlantic duty elimination even in these sectors should not cause severe adjustment problems for members or nonmembers.

Richard Baldwin and Joseph Francois have estimated that the elimination of remaining tariffs on nonagricultural products between NAFTA and the EU/EFTA (European Free Trade Agreement) will increase trade by only 1.5 percent, with consequent income gains ranging from no change to 0.1 percent.[2] These estimates do not take full account of dynamic growth effects, such as increased international investment stimulated by tariff elimination, which could double or triple the overall gains, but the net result in any event is modest positive effects for TAFTA members and a very small adverse impact on nonmembers.

Additional gains in trade and growth would result from the inclusion of other trade-related policy commitments within a TAFTA. Much activity is already underway in these areas of policy. Negotiation of an OECD agreement on investment policy would establish a basic framework for investment which could be strengthened over time within a TAFTA. Important issues such as competition policy, government procurement, industrial standards, and intellectual property rights are engaged bilaterally between the United States and the EU, principally as a result of the New Transatlantic Agenda adopted at a summit meeting in Madrid in December 1995.[3] An initial priority for the Agenda has been regulatory cooperation: "We aim to achieve an agreement on mutual recognition of conformity assessment (which includes certification and testing procedures) for certain sectors as soon as possible." Much of the work on such agreements and other areas of technical cooperation is being done by the parallel private sector body, the Transatlantic Business Dialogue. By 1997 mutual recognition agreements had been completed or were near completion for seven sectors, including pharmaceuticals, telecommunications, and medical equipment. A structured TAFTA should facilitate progress in all of these trade-related policy areas so as to achieve the "New Transatlantic Marketplace" objective contained in the Madrid summit declaration.

Agriculture has long been the bane of transatlantic trade relations, but even here circumstances are decidedly more favorable than they were in the 1980s and earlier. Again, the Uruguay Round agreement provided a breakthrough. The European Common Agricultural Policy (CAP) of variable import levies and unlimited export subsidies was fundamentally restructured as a system of fixed tariffs (cut by 36 percent), including greater use of income support payments for farmers where necessary and reductions in export subsidies of 21–36 percent from earlier levels. The Uruguay Round also commits governments to negotiate further liberalization in agricultural trade within five years, which would fit the scenario for a TAFTA negotiation. Further liberalization of agricultural trade is also more propitious at this juncture because rising world grain prices and a drawdown in stocks would limit adverse impact on farmers. In addition, the European political imperative to bring Central and Eastern European countries into the EU, beginning with at least Poland, Hungary, and the Czech Republic, is currently inhibited by the potential costs of the existing farm policy, which a TAFTA initiative could serve to alleviate.

It is difficult to predict what precise form of agricultural agreement would emerge from a TAFTA negotiation. Complete free trade would be a long-term commitment at best. A related WTO multilateral commitment for reductions in export subsidies and MFN tariffs, patterned on Uruguay Round reductions, would be well-received by nonmember exporting countries.

Elimination of tariffs on agricultural products traded largely across the Atlantic, with precedent from the existing free trade agreements between the EU and Central European countries, would move the trade relationship substantially closer to free trade. Whether such an overall arrangement would be in reasonable conformance with Article XXIV of the GATT, which requires elimination of border restrictions on "substantially all the trade" among members of a free trade agreement, would depend on the specific results. Only about 5 percent of transatlantic trade is in agricultural products to begin with, and if much or most of this could be subject to a phaseout of tariffs among TAFTA members, such conformity would be justified.

Baldwin and Francois made a further estimate of the trade impact of a TAFTA which included, in addition to tariff elimination on nonagricultural products, substantial liberalization or harmonization in trade-related policies, including competition policy, government procurement, and standards, and the elimination of agricultural protection. On this basis, transatlantic trade increases by 4–5 percent and income by 0.3 percent, but again without taking full account of the dynamic gains from trade which might take on even greater relative importance in the context of such a comprehensive free trade relationship.

The net assessment of the trade effects of a TAFTA is that they would be moderate in scope and reasonably balanced across the Atlantic. The transatlantic trade and investment relationship is mature and balanced to begin with. The economic gains from trade would benefit consumers on both sides of the Atlantic, while the much larger and more open transatlantic market would make both North American and European firms more efficient vis-à-vis competitors in other regions, particularly East Asia. Moreover, protectionist concerns in the United States and Europe about cheap labor and inadequate environmental standards in developing countries would simply not apply, making political support for a TAFTA easier to obtain.

Impact on the International Trading System

This has been the most hotly debated aspect of a TAFTA, but thus far it has been an inadequate debate. A TAFTA has been posed either negatively as undercutting the WTO by expanding preferential trade on a regional basis at the expense of multilateral, MFN commitments in the WTO, or positively as one further building block toward more open overall trade.[4] In fact, a

TAFTA would have far greater impact on the trading system than these antipodal outcomes imply, and could lead to a broader transformation of the system based on global free trade. The full effects cannot be judged by examining a TAFTA in isolation. An assessment must include its dynamic impact on other parts of the trading system, regional as well as multilateral.

A relatively quickly negotiated TAFTA over the next several years, and including an OECD investment agreement, should facilitate the broadening of regional free trade already engaged in Europe and the Western Hemisphere. The TAFTA would almost certainly have to be open-ended to provide entry for European and Western Hemisphere countries as they proceed to negotiate membership in the EU and the 2005 target date for free trade in the Western Hemisphere approaches. Indeed, these countries should welcome the opportunity to join in the broader transatlantic grouping and not have to choose between Europe and North America. The receptivity of Mexico and the South American Mercosur grouping to free trade overtures from the EU is an indication of such a positive disposition, while Poland and other Central European countries would surely welcome an extended free trade relationship with the United States.

The Asia-Pacific relationship is more critical to the overall outcome for the world trading system and is also more complicated, requiring a premium on commercial diplomacy and statesmanship. The key would be to move forward with the 2010 commitment for free trade by the more advanced APEC nations—the United States, Canada, Mexico, Japan, Australia and New Zealand, and possibly South Korea, Singapore, Taiwan, and Hong Kong—while reaching a longer-term arrangement with the less-advanced members, including China. The response of Japan, South Korea and the ASEAN members would be especially important, and the mere beginning of formal consideration of a TAFTA between the United States and the EU should provide a stimulus for these East Asian countries to focus more precisely on how to achieve free trade and investment objective across the Pacific or, more broadly, within the WTO. This subject is examined in greater detail in essay 5.

The ultimate result for the trading system, stemming from the catalytic effects of a TAFTA initiative, could—and should—be a broad and preponderant free trade and investment relationship, comprising Europe and the Western Hemisphere, extended to the more advanced East Asian economies, and open to other major trading nations as they become willing and able to join. This is the multilateral/regional synthesis presented in greater detail in essay 6, which would entail far-reaching consequences for the trading system. The impact on the WTO as an institution would be substantial and would go beyond simply depositing documents in Geneva based on GATT Article XXIV. A dichotomy between the dominant core of members engaged in a comprehensive free trade relationship—including 75 percent or more of world trade—and the many other members, almost all developing countries, would require some changes in the WTO structure. The concept of conditional MFN, long anathema to the GATT, although with a significant exception in the Uruguay Round agreement on public procurement, would have to be reconsidered. So, too, the one member, one vote decision-making procedure, which is the political Achilles' heel of the WTO. The end result, however, should be a more durable and responsive multilateral trade organization based on free trade and investment.

The Foreign Policy Consequences

This is by far the least-discussed dimension of a TAFTA, but in the end it could be the most important. Proponents of a TAFTA, including leaders with a more strategic vision of global economic relationships, proclaim the foreign policy benefits of bringing the NATO allies, or more broadly the Western industrialized democracies, closer together through a politically high-profile transatlantic free trade agreement. They also stress the potential divisiveness of Europe and North America drifting apart into rival economic blocs, which would be avoided through a TAFTA. Beyond such obvious direct benefits of a TAFTA, however, there has been little serious attention given as to how such a strengthened and broadened world trading system would synergize and interact with broader post–Cold War political and security objectives. Such an analysis also goes beyond the scope of this presentation, and all that is offered is one general observation and two particular examples of how a broad-based free trade grouping, including a comprehensive free trade commitment across the Atlantic, could provide a more stable and secure world political order.

The general observation is that the evolution of the international trade and investment system as projected above, and given impulse by a TAFTA initiative, would place the industrialized democracy grouping more prominently at the center of the broader world order, and in position to extend in membership and deepen in content over time. It would be a cooperative relationship based on the rapidly growing gains from international trade and investment. In this context, common interests with respect to so-called rogue states, such as North Korea, Iran, and Libya, or failing nation states in crisis, such as Bosnia, Haiti, and Somalia, could be addressed more effectively.

The two particular examples are Russia and China. If Russian economic and political reforms move forward, it is only a matter of a relatively short time before Russia—and Ukraine—request a preferential trade agreement with the EU, based on the already existing EU free trade arrangements with Poland and other Central European countries. Ukraine is already associated with the Central European free trade grouping, with explicit aspirations for EU linkages, and the EU has agreed to discuss free trade with Russia as early as 1998 if Russian economic reforms continue to move forward. An EU-Russian free trade agreement, in particular, would be attractive to Russian, French, and other European nationalists seeking to reestablish Europe—from the Atlantic to the Urals—as a world power independent from the United States. In any event, Russian exports to Europe on a preferential basis compared with U.S. exports would create a political problem in Washington. A TAFTA would preclude any such dilemma while facilitating a transition of Russia into a broadened North Atlantic relationship as circumstances permit.

Integrating China into the world community, based on open markets and democratization, is the greatest challenge to the post–Cold War political as well as economic order. A consolidation of regional free trade agreements among the industrialized democracies, with prominent impetus through a TAFTA, would likely be viewed as threatening to some in Beijing, and a carefully crafted strategy would be needed to convince them otherwise. The starting points for explaining a TAFTA in positive terms to China and other Asian trading partners would be to point out that a TAFTA would do nothing more than achieve the free trade objective already engaged across the Pacific between North America and East Asia, and that the North Atlantic nations, as the most open and industrialized economies, should be among the first rather than the last regions to eliminate remaining restrictions to trade. The conclusion drawn here is that a consolidated free trade approach, including a TAFTA, should offer greater opportunity to deal effectively and constructively with the Chinese politico-economic relationship than would the existing, relatively weak WTO and APEC forums alone. Needless to say, this conclusion deserves special scrutiny in a more detailed evaluation of the impact of a TAFTA on broader geostrategic interests.

First Steps

Indeed, a thorough analysis of all of the above aspects of the rationale for NAFTA constitutes a necessary precondition for launching a TAFTA initiative, but North Atlantic governments have thus far been hesitant if not opposed to doing so. Public interest in a TAFTA began in 1994, coming first from European leaders and Canadian Prime Minister Jean Chrétien. The first Clinton administration, however, was decidedly cool to the idea, already engaged with free trade commitments in the Western Hemisphere and APEC and faced with growing protectionist criticism of NAFTA in the wake of the Mexican financial crisis. In June 1995, EU Commissioner Leon Brittan raised the TAFTA issue with Secretary of State Warren Christopher, who went no further than to promise it "serious study."

The opportunity for serious study of a TAFTA came during preparations for the December 1995 U.S.-EU summit in Madrid, which established the New Transatlantic Agenda, but both sides decided not to pursue it in favor of an action program of specific steps to facilitate trade and investment short of free trade. French opposition within the EU and U.S. reluctance to take on any new trade initiatives in an election year were sufficient to at least postpone official examination of a TAFTA. The disinterest in a TAFTA was especially ironic in that in the week before the Madrid meeting EU foreign ministers agreed to a work program, including free trade by 2010, with twelve Middle East and North African countries, and in the week after Madrid an EU commissioner agreed to joint preparations for a free trade area with the Mercosur countries of South America. Transatlantic trade thus became an even more conspicuous odd person out in the rapidly evolving regional free trade scheme of things.

Initial U.S. official disinterest in a TAFTA will not, however, be the last word on the subject. The decisive phase for its consideration begins as the second Clinton administration formulates its overall trade strategy and its relationship with Europe in particular. The New Transatlantic Agenda of December 1995, including the creation of a New Transatlantic Marketplace, is sweeping in its intent: "For the last 50 years, the transatlantic relationship has been central to the security and prosperity of our people. Our aspirations for the future must surpass our achievements in the past." Surely, surpassing fifty years of past achievements must involve something more than a few mutual recognition agreements on certification and testing procedures.

An indirect reference to a possible TAFTA in the December 1995 summit statement was contained in the commitment to carry out, "a joint study on ways of facilitating trade in goods and services and further reducing or eliminating tariff and non-tariff barriers." This is a considerable dilution of Secretary Christopher's agreement six months earlier to give a TAFTA serious consideration. A study of tariff and nontariff barrier elimination is only one narrow technical aspect of a TAFTA. Moreover, as of late 1997, even this technical study had still not been completed. Interest in a TAFTA, however, continues to broaden, including prominent European leaders, such as former U.K. Prime Minister Margaret Thatcher and German Foreign Minister Klaus Kinkel, and members of the U.S. Congress, including Senator Richard Lugar and Congressman Lee Hamilton.[5] At a minimum, a full and serious study of a TAFTA should be undertaken. It would begin with an assessment of the direct trade impact from the elimination of border restrictions and greater harmony of trade-related domestic policies, which should produce mutual, though modest, benefits, with little adverse impact on nonmember trading partners. The full foreign policy implications should be assessed, drawing on the judgments of political leaders on both sides of the Atlantic. And the ramifications of a TAFTA on the evolution of the international trading system, particularly the relationship between regional free trade objectives and the slower moving trade liberalization process within the multilateral WTO, would need to be factored in.

The immediate issue is how to get this serious evaluation started as early as possible so as to lay the groundwork for a formal TAFTA initiative within the next couple of years. To this end, four specific steps are suggested:

1. The North Atlantic governments should be exhorted at every opportunity to undertake a serious, comprehensive evaluation of the mutual interests in a TAFTA. In the United States, Secretary of State Madeleine Albright should be urged to follow through on former Secretary Christopher's earlier commitment. It is irresponsible for the United States and the EU to refuse even to evaluate the issue when each is pursuing free trade with various other regions of the world.

2. Private sector leaders should undertake their own assessment of the impact of a TAFTA on investment, job creation, new technology development, corporate restructuring, and the generally more productive private sectors that free and open competition across the Atlantic would generate. The Transatlantic Business Dialogue, composed of a large number of CEOs on both sides of the Atlantic, have thus far avoided the issue and concentrated on more immediate, technical objectives, but they should now put TAFTA formally on their agenda.

3. Interparliamentary dialogue should be engaged across the Atlantic. Members of legislatures on both continents need to participate in order to understand the benefits of a TAFTA and to be able to communicate actively about them with constituents.

4. An Eminent Persons Group (EPG) should be established to analyze the full implications of a TAFTA and to make recommendations. This would follow the precedent of the APEC initiative, in which a nongovernmental EPG, led by the American economist Fred Bergsten, galvanized support for the free trade goal in the face of initial resistance from governments. An EPG for a TAFTA, however, would play a qualitatively different role. The Bergsten group, comprised mostly of economists and technocrats, became primarily engaged in the very challenging technical modalities of eliminating trade barriers for highly disparate national economies and continues to play this role in advising government leaders. An EPG for a TAFTA, in contrast, would concentrate on the broader systemic and strategic implications at stake, since the direct trade issues involved are relatively straight forward, and the EPG would be limited to a single report. The EPG should thus consist of distinguished private and former public sector leaders on both sides of the Atlantic.

The time has come for serious and sympathetic consideration of a TAFTA. The rapid recent course of world events, including the growing relative importance of economic relationships and the potential momentum for regional free trade agreements in Europe, the Americas, and across the Pacific, dictate the need for a more closely knit North Atlantic economic relationship. The New Transatlantic Agenda recognizes this in rhetorical terms, but lacks substance. The most evident substantive response would be to create a TAFTA. All that is lacking is the initiative to begin a TAFTA initiative.

4

Regulatory Regimes in World Trade: The Case of NAFTA and the FTAA

The world trading system has been expanding in policy scope at both the multilateral and regional levels. The Uruguay Round agreement greatly expanded the scope of the multilateral system to include trade in services and intellectual property rights (IPRs); to extend commitments in such areas as agriculture, standards, and public procurement; and to propose a future work program for the WTO in such areas as investment and competition policies, as well as the trade policy relationships with environmental and perhaps labor standards. At the regional level, the EU is well-advanced toward economic and monetary union, covering a wide range of trade-related policies, while NAFTA, although less inclusive than the EU, also goes well beyond the current coverage of WTO commitments.

This rapidly expanding scope of trade-related commitments involves, to a far greater extent than adjustments in tariff levels and other border restrictions to trade, national regulatory policies, or "regulatory regimes" as referred to here. A more complex set of definitions, standards, and implementation procedures is brought into play, with deeper interaction between domestic and foreign firms. National treatment is usually the starting point and the ultimate goal can be harmonized systems or mutual recognition agreements (MRAs), but the current state of the trading system with respect to regulatory regimes consists, for the most part, of something in between, ill-defined and even less-clearly implemented.

This essay addresses evolving trade relationships within the Western Hemisphere, in particular the implementation of NAFTA and Mercosur and preparations for a Free Trade Agreement of the Americas (FTAA) by 2005. Attention is focused on the regulatory provisions in key areas of policy within this framework, and the overarching policy question is whether this largely separate regional institutional setting is on a divergent or convergent path vis-à-vis other institutional bases for trade, principally the WTO at the multilateral level and the expanding EU regional grouping; in effect, are these rival or mutually reinforcing regulatory regimes?

The central conclusion is that the free trade course in the Western Hemisphere, with one notable exception, is highly compatible with the trade-liberalizing objectives of the WTO, including the required regulatory frameworks, and that indeed it is playing a path-breaking role in several key areas of strengthening and extending the multilateral trading system. The prospect for the NAFTA/FTAA relationship with the European Union is less clear and is contingent on what happens within Europe and in the New Transatlantic Agenda launched at the December 1995 summit meeting in Madrid.

The essay begins with a discussion of the broad policy context within which the Western Hemisphere free trade objective is developing, and then examines, in greater detail, nine specific areas of policy where free trade commitments or objectives are deeply intertwined with national regulatory policies. The final section draws conclusions about regulatory regimes and trade liberalizing policy objectives.

The Broad Policy Context

The current quest for free trade within the Western Hemisphere has three characteristics—political orientation, trade policy decision-making, and the bridging of the North-South divide—which bear critically on the relationship with the WTO, each in a mutually reinforcing direction. All three characteristics, moreover, are distinct from circumstances within the EU, which has implications for the course of the overall world trading system.

Political Orientation

NAFTA and the FTAA initiative have an explicit political objective of supporting democratic governments in the Hemisphere through higher economic growth and more decentralized, private-sector-oriented societies inherent in free trade relationships. This objective, however, is indirect and does not involve the goal of political integration beyond the separate, largely consultative framework of the Organization of American States (OAS). The motivation of Canada and Mexico for NAFTA was, in fact, to secure enhanced access to their dominant export market—the United States—without unduly sacrificing national sovereignty, and a similar commercial, as distinct from political, motivation exists elsewhere in the Hemisphere with respect to an FTAA. In this context, WTO commitments are viewed as mutually reinforcing to those obtained within NAFTA/FTAA, such as for dispute settlement and safeguards, as a means of resisting protectionist actions in the United States, and assuring free market access. The United States, in turn, views NAFTA and FTAA as of both commercial and foreign policy benefit, but only as one part of a global trade strategy including, in comparable status, Asia and Europe, and with the WTO as the vital multilateral foundation. The U.S. record is less clear than for others in the Hemisphere as to whether regional free trade is a "building block" for broader free trade or a "strategic economic bloc" of more mercantilist character, but the discussion of specific issues below indicates that, in practice, the "building block" goal is almost always paramount.

The EU, in contrast, has always had the objective of some form of political integration within Europe, which has become more explicit over the years and is addressed even more comprehensively within the 1996 Inter-Governmental Conference. There is also no question that economic as well as political relationships within Europe are primus inter pares compared with relations with other regions (with the notable exception, at least until recently, of the NATO security relationship), and that WTO commitments, while important, do not necessarily take precedence over steps toward economic union within Europe.

Trade Policy Decision-Making

Following from the NAFTA political context of minimizing the cessation of national sovereignty, trade policy decision-making has not been integrated, and implementation of NAFTA takes place through consultative bodies and dispute settlement mechanisms that expand on but do not displace the already strengthened multilateral consultative and dispute mechanisms of the WTO. Technical secretariats on an integrated basis have been almost entirely avoided. The FTAA outlook is not yet clear with respect to formal structure, including the need for an integrated secretariat, but member nations will almost certainly seek maximum freedom to pursue an independent trade policy course, most importantly within the WTO. This freedom would be constrained only to a limited extent in the unlikely event that the FTAA takes the form of a customs union, in whole or for some sectors, whereby adjustments in the common external tariff would have to be jointly agreed.

Again in contrast, the EU has had integrated trade policy decision-making from the outset, implemented through complex intergovernmental and supranational mechanisms, with the supranational EU Commission representing all members, with a single voice, within the WTO. This integration of trade policy goes well beyond the common external tariff and continues to expand as the EU broadens its internal authorities toward economic and monetary union and the WTO extends its policy scope as a result of the Uruguay Round agreement and its post–Uruguay Round agenda.

Bridging the North-South Divide

The most important characteristic as to how free trade within the Western Hemisphere is influencing the overall trading system is what can be called the bridging of the North-South divide. NAFTA involves a comprehensive free trade agreement between two major industrialized countries and one major developing country, based almost entirely on fully reciprocal commitments. Mexico, in its own self-interest, opened its market to a far greater degree than did the United States and Canada because its tariffs and other border restrictions were much higher to begin with, and new commitments in such areas as investment, intellectual property rights, transportation, and public procurement were far more consequential for Mexico. The sharp distinction between industrialized and developing countries which permeated the GATT and now the WTO, with a contentious history over preferential or "special and differential" treatment, simply does not exist within NAFTA. Moreover, the outlook for an FTAA is essentially to continue this nonspecial, nondifferential relationship. Even the small economies of the Caribbean Basin region are likely to receive special treatment, for the most part, in terms of a longer timeframe for implementing free trade commitments. This regional integration on a nonpreferential basis will have substantial impact on the future course of the WTO, hopefully leading to its becoming a truly multilateral framework of reciprocal market access commitments.

In contrast, the EU is far less relevant in its impact on North-South relationships within the WTO. The EU is predominantly a free trade arrangement among industrialized countries, with the less developed members, such as Greece and Portugal, at the periphery. Moreover, EU integration includes an integral component of regional subsidies from more advanced to less advanced members and regions within member states, an indirect form of special and differential treatment.

In sum, the process of moving toward comprehensive free trade within the Western Hemisphere is not only compatible with the continued evolution of the multilateral WTO, but a leading-edge force for global free trade, most conspicuously through bridging the dichotomy between industrialized and developing countries that has long been a hallmark of the GATT/WTO. This leading edge role, moreover, can also influence other less advanced regional initiatives, such as the APEC 2020 free trade objective. How the Western Hemisphere process is playing out is evident in specific policy areas being implemented within NAFTA and developed at the prenegotiation stage for an FTAA. Much of it concerns the reform and strengthening of regulatory practices, where WTO, NAFTA and prospective FTAA commitments tend especially to overlap. The following section illustrates both the scope and complexity of this challenge.

Specific Policy Areas

An interactive evolution of trade policy commitments within the WTO, NAFTA, and the FTAA initiative exists in almost all areas of trade-related policies, but the significance and intensity of the interaction varies greatly among specific policy areas, including impact on national regulatory regimes. The following presentation summarizes this interaction in nine areas of policy keyed to the working groups established within the FTAA framework.[1] The discussion traces the working group deliberations through the May 1997 ministerial meeting in Belo Horizonte, Brazil, as preparation for the summit meeting to launch formal negotiations to be held in Santiago, Chile, in April 1998. There are, in fact, twelve such working groups, but three groups have been excluded. The Working Group on Market Access has been excluded in part because it focuses on elimination of border restrictions rather than regulatory practices, and in part because it is simply too wideranging in scope to be addressed here. In the agricultural sector, for example, the elimination of border restrictions—as has been largely accomplished within NAFTA— involves a wide range of regulatory consequences that are only partially addressed here in terms of sanitary and phytosanitary measures and export subsidies. The second excluded working group, for "smaller economies," deals with broader, generic issues of transition to free trade for such economies rather than specific areas of policy commitments. The third excluded working group concerns dispute settlement, which only began work in July 1997 with an unclear mandate. The nine included policy areas are presented in the order in which they are listed within the FTAA work program, with the first five having been established at the June 1995 ministerial meeting in Denver, Colorado, and the final four at the March 1996 meeting in Cartagena, Colombia.

Policy Area 1: Customs Procedures and Rules of Origin

Policy area 1 is very broad in scope and has two components. For the first component, customs procedures, the FTAA working group is charged with developing a complete inventory and a transparent system of customs procedures, achieving technical cooperation in customs administration (including linked computer systems), simplifying customs procedures, and composing guidelines for the preparation of a basic common nomenclature conforming to the International Harmonized System. All of this involves close cooperation and regulatory institution-building which is highly supportive of parallel work underway within the WTO. The second component, rules of origin, is far more controversial and is, in fact, the "one notable exception" to the otherwise trade-liberalizing result of NAFTA referred to in the previous section.

Rules of origin are used to determine the country of origin for imported goods where national origin has some bearing on the treatment of imports. The basic definition of national origin is the country where the last "substantial transformation" of the product took place. Three criteria for determining this have been utilized within the GATT trading system for nonpreferential trade: a change in tariff classification, the percentage of value added, and the location of particular manufacturing or processing operations. The Uruguay Round agreement defined these criteria more clearly and established a three-year work program to harmonize the application of rules of origin, with precedence for the criterion of change in tariff classification, and with a view to ensuring that "rules of origin shall not themselves create restrictive, distorting or disruptive effects on international trade." This WTO mandate was undertaken with the realization that the strong trend toward a greater international division of production, especially for technology-intensive industries, can make country of origin tests exceedingly complex and costly. The process of documenting value added, in particular, can be very costly for importers, require additional customs inspectors, and provide lucrative legal fees when the process is challenged by import-competing domestic industries.

A rules of origin test has also been accepted in the GATT for free trade agreements in order to prevent goods being imported into the lower tariff member of the free trade agreement for re-export, duty-free, to the higher tariff member. Curiously, however, the conditions for such a rules of origin test within a free trade area have not been elaborated or even mentioned in GATT Article XXIV, which provides for the creation of free trade areas, and the Uruguay Round agreement on rules of origin is limited to nonpreferential trade. It is thus in this gray area of ill-defined applicability of ill-defined rules of origin tests that NAFTA, and now the FTAA work program, have been operating. Regrettably, the NAFTA result was highly abusive of the concept underlying the need for a rules of origin test, with consequent trade-restrictive, -distorting, and -disruptive effects, and the NAFTA precedent may now spill over to the outcome for the FTAA as well as the WTO work program.

The NAFTA rules of origin outcome is a consequence of a basically flawed concept and of application of the three test criteria in a more restrictive manner than normal practice up to this point. The flawed concept relates to the self-evident fact that if a rules of origin test within a free trade area is to prevent circumvention through importing into the low tariff country for re-export to high tariff country, then only the high tariff country should be permitted to apply a rules of origin test.[2] Moreover, there should be some minimal tariff differential requirement to offset the inherent transshipment costs from the low to high tariff country. On this basis, the United States would have little need to apply a rules of origin test on imports from Mexico within NAFTA since Mexican tariffs are generally much higher than U.S. tariffs.

Nevertheless, the United States insisted on elaborate, costly rules of origin testing. For the automotive sector, the customary 50 percent value added criterion was increased to 62.5 percent in a blatant effort to restrict production by Japanese auto manufacturers in Mexico and is related to parallel domestic content performance requirements being pressed upon Japanese transplant operations in the United States.[3] NAFTA also permits in some sectors greater flexibility for the tariff-heading criterion (for example, a shift of tariff classification from the customary four digit level to the two digit level, which becomes a more difficult test), and the cumulation of criteria: change of tariff classification *and* minimal value added *and* specific manufacturing or processing operation.

This trade-inhibiting NAFTA shadow now falls over the FTAA work program. Elsewhere in the region, the longstanding Latin American Integration Association (ALADI) free trade agreements simply require a four digit tariff heading change *or* 50 percent regional value added. Mercosur adopted a four digit change *or* 60 percent value added—the 60 percent level at Brazilian insistence. Recent Mexican free trade agreements with Venezuela and Colombia—the G-3 agreement—and elsewhere in the Hemisphere follow the more restrictive NAFTA criteria. Many economists not disposed to regional free trade agreements in the first place decry the proliferation of overlapping rules of origin provisions throughout the world as a regulatory nightmare. They have a good point to which the FTAA working group needs to respond.

It is not clear how the rules of origin negotiations will shape up within the FTAA. One minimal constraint would be to adhere to the outcome of the three-year WTO mandate to develop a harmonized system. There has also been informal discussion of seeking common tariff levels throughout the Hemisphere in given sectors which would negate rules of origin testing in these sectors. This is commendable, but, in addition, the bolder, common sense requirement—whereby only the higher tariff country can apply rules or origin, with a minimum percent differential to offset the transshipment cost—should be adopted.

Policy Area 2: Investment

In contrast with the trade-restrictive orientation of the rules of origin issue, investment policy is the outstanding example of how free trade in the Western Hemisphere is at the leading edge for broadening the scope of the multilateral trading system, principally with respect to the industrialized/developing country relationship, thereby increasing the likelihood that the WTO will become a WTIO—World Trade and Investment Organization—within the next five to ten years.

The Uruguay Round agreement includes two significant but limited commitments for bringing foreign investment policy within the WTO. The trade-related investment measures (TRIMs) agreement restricts the use of some performance requirements for foreign investment, such as domestic content and trade-balancing requirements, and commits the WTO to reconsider within five years broader commitments for investment policy, for which a working party was established at the December 1996 Singapore ministerial meeting. More important, the Uruguay Round agreement on trade in services involves, ipso facto, an agreement on international investment because the provision of services usually requires an investment-based presence in country. The shortcomings of the Uruguay Round services agreement, as explained more fully under policy area 8 below, are that sectoral coverage is limited in most developing countries and that liberalization of existing access for foreign investors was left for future negotiation.

Momentum is now building for more comprehensive investment agreements, mostly because developing countries and former as well as remaining communist countries are actively encouraging foreign direct investment as a central component of national development strategy. A multilateral investment agreement is under negotiation within the OECD. Bilateral investment treaties (BITs) continue to be negotiated as they have over several decades. The APEC organization adopted a voluntary—and disappointingly weak—code of conduct for international investment in 1995. The most dramatic breakthrough in the 1990s, however, has been in the Western Hemisphere in NAFTA and other subregional agreements, now all feeding into the FTAA initiative.

NAFTA Chapter 11 is a comprehensive investment agreement that has become the model for the OECD negotiation as well as the benchmark for a maximum FTAA outcome. The NAFTA agreement includes national treatment; prohibition of expropriation except for public purposes and then only with prompt and effective compensation; free transfer of profits abroad; a related U.S.-Mexico tax treaty; greater restriction on performance requirements than contained in the Uruguay Round TRIMs agreement; and recourse for investors to binding arbitration of disputes under international rules such as those of the World Bank International Center for the Settlement of Investment Disputes (ICSID) and the UN Commission on International Trade Laws (UNCITRAL). Of central importance, the right of establishment is broad in scope, including all sectors except narrowly defined exceptions, principally the energy and railroad sectors in Mexico, airline and radio communication in the United States, and Canadian cultural industries, plus a screening process for very large investments in Mexico and Canada.[4] Financial, telecommunications, and transportation services are included within NAFTA in terms of progressive liberalization targets for foreign investors.

Elsewhere in the Western Hemisphere, subregional investment agreements have been adopted largely consistent with NAFTA. The Mercosur protocol on investment is relatively general but does include the automatic right of establishment, or "admission," except for explicitly reserved sectors. Mexican bilateral free trade agreements with Colombia, Venezuela, Costa Rica and Bolivia include investment provisions close to Chapter 11 of NAFTA, and the 1991 bilateral investment treaty between the United States and Argentina establishes a significant link between NAFTA and Mercosur.

As a consequence of this momentum toward incorporating broad-based investment provisions in subregional agreements, the FTAA working group report to the March 1996 Cartagena meeting was the most forthcoming of all, recommending that an FTAA "incorporate the subject of investment into the agreement." A number of specific areas of convergence are elaborated, including most of the principles contained in NAFTA, and six principal areas of difference are listed as a focus for further working group examination: different legal traditions, the definition and scope of the foreign investment concept, the application of the right of establishment, incentives to foreign investors, and the scope of sectors open to foreign investment. Further technical work on these specific issues was presented at Belo Horizonte in May 1997, at which time the Business Forum of the Americas put forward a set of proposals calling for an investment agreement to be "one of the first accomplishments of the FTAA process"—yet another example of private sector leadership for free trade.

The implications of such a broad-based investment agreement for regulatory regimes are far-reaching, including the learning process within the existing subregional and bilateral agreements and the FTAA working group deliberations. NAFTA is being implemented with positive momentum, particularly as Mexico seeks to improve its investment climate in the wake of the 1995 financial crisis. The transition period for foreign investor access to the Mexican banking sector has been accelerated as has the scope of investment for enhanced value added services in the telecommunications sector. Consultation on tax provisions and legal adaptation of investment commitments, including at state and provincial levels, to prevent discrimination against foreign investors is generally cooperative, although some problems have surfaced. Arbitrated dispute settlement by an international body has not yet been tested.

The FTAA process of assessing the need for regulatory reform and convergence is an important preparatory stage to formal negotiation of an investment agreement. Reports prepared for the working group, "Compendium of Bilateral Investment Treaties in the Western Hemisphere" and "Regulations of Foreign Investment in the Trade and Integration Agreements of the Western Hemisphere," form the starting point for more detailed preparations for a hemispheric agreement, with the six areas of difference noted above as regulatory-heavy priority subjects.[5] Looking ahead, the ultimate shape of an investment agreement within an FTAA will likely depend heavily on the scope of exclusions from a right of establishment commitment, particularly between NAFTA maximum inclusion and what Mercosur countries are likely to accept. In the meantime, the learning process, especially for the smaller and less-developed countries, will be important not only for reaching a comprehensive investment agreement of broad scope within the Western Hemisphere, but for laying the groundwork for a later multilateral agreement on investment in the WTO.

Policy Area 3: Standards and Technical Barriers to Trade

The administration of product, professional, and other technical standards is almost totally involved with national regulatory regimes and is of increasing importance as production processes become more technologically complex. Two-thirds of complaints brought before the WTO dispute settlement mechanism during its first two years of operation involved technical standards, including the first dispute panel finding against the United States on reformulated gasoline imports, wherein environmental standards for imports were judged discriminatory, or not in compliance with the national treatment commitment. In a more positive direction, cooperative actions in this area involve greater transparency in establishing and administering standards and efforts to achieve internationally harmonized standards or MRAs. Harmonization is pursued in the International Standards Organization (ISO) and other forums, principally among industrialized countries. The Uruguay Round agreement provides greater specificity than the earlier GATT code with respect to standards, regulatory practices, and conformity assessment procedures (e.g., registration, inspection, and laboratory assessment), and establishes a work program to assure implementation. The Uruguay Round agreement is noteworthy in that all developing country members of the WTO are parties to the agreement, in contrast to the prior voluntary GATT code, which was limited almost entirely to industrialized country signatories.

Progress to date for implementing the Uruguay Round agreement in the area of technical standards has been modest, but it is expected to accelerate over time. The WTO work program will serve as a learning and institution-building process for developing countries while the 1995 Transatlantic Business Dialogue initiative puts a high priority on harmonized technical standards and MRAs. OECD and APEC agendas also include active work on technical standards, and NAFTA/FTAA activities provide additional impetus, particularly with respect to developing country participation.

NAFTA provides not only a consultative process for greater transparency and specification of standards, of particular relevance in Mexico, but also specific targets for harmonization of standards and MRAs. NAFTA specifies a work program for harmonization of common standards in the telecommunications, automotive, land transportation, and textile and apparel sectors. MRAs are in place or targeted for various services. Actual progress in these harmonization efforts will move slowly and can be controversial, but the process is officially engaged and cross-border enterprises in all three member nations have an interest in more transparent, simplified, and harmonized standards.

The FTAA process starts at a much more rudimentary level. There is little collaboration among Mercosur countries on standards up to this point, although a longstanding structure in Central America among members of the Central American Common Market (CACM) provides a model for smaller countries. The FTAA Working Group on Standards mandate is highly explicit about how its work program will be directly supportive and mutually reinforcing to the WTO work program, with eight specific references to the Uruguay Round agreement and the WTO. The first steps for developing a more open system of standards are to establish a transparent notification procedure for standards and an "inquiry point" within governments for questions about standards. By 1996, such inquiry points had been established in only twelve out of thirty-four FTAA participants. An initial "Inventory of National Practices on Standards, Technical Regulations and Conformity Assessment in the Western Hemisphere" was prepared for the working group, and its 1996–97 work program objectives include examining the principles, concepts, and requirements of MRAs for conformity assessment procedures, organizing subregional seminars, developing written material on implementation for specified issues, examining the provisions and actions under existing subregional trading arrangements, and exploring the possibility of developing computerized hemispheric information systems.

Overarching the field of technical standards is a basic difference in orientation between the United States and most of the rest of the world. The U.S. approach is for the private sector to take the lead in developing regulations for standards on the grounds that companies are better informed than governments as to evolving technical requirements and options for harmonized standards. The United States, for example, is the only country represented in the ISO by the private sector. Almost all other countries, in contrast, develop regulated technical standards with greater initiative from government bodies. The accelerating pace of technological change and the growing complexity of setting reasonable standards, however, is moving the process in the direction of the American approach, with greater private sector participation. For the Western Hemisphere, the relationship between governments and the private sector in developing standards regulations thus needs to be defined more clearly, with a more prominent and direct private sector participation than has existed in the FTAA process up to this point.

How this will all play out in the period ahead, within the WTO, among the industrialized countries bilaterally or through the OECD, across the Pacific within APEC, and within the Western Hemisphere, is far from clear. The role of NAFTA/FTAA, however, is distinct and important for two reasons. First, it will almost certainly remain scrupulously supportive of the multilateral WTO process. And second, it will play a catalytic role for developing countries: in the case of Mexico, in actively negotiating harmonized standards and MRAs with its dominant industrialized trading partners, and, for all others in the Hemisphere, initially acting as a critical institution-building process for establishing more open and predictable national regulatory regimes for technical standards.

Policy Area 4: Sanitary and Phytosanitary Measures

Policy area 4 is, in effect, a subset of standards involving trade controls to protect human, animal, or plant life or health, which has had a troubled trade policy history of protectionist abuse, and for which the Uruguay Round agreement established a more harmonized international regulatory system based on "scientific principles." The agreement encourages the development and use of international standards but permits stricter national standards "if there is scientific justification." A critical element of the system is a risk assessment test which precludes longstanding practices of "zero tolerance" whereby, for example, all imports of a farm product from the United States can be permanently banned if one medfly is uncovered in a remote corner of California. This policy area faces a number of specific problems, particularly among industrialized countries, and involves relatively weak to almost nonexistent regulatory regimes in developing countries. Both industrialized and developing countries are engaged in initial WTO activities. The United States, for example, is challenging the EU ban on imports of American hormone-fed beef on the grounds that a scientific justification is lacking, while the WTO is organizing a work program to help developing countries build more transparent and scientifically based regulatory procedures.

The NAFTA and FTAA initiative are both deeply involved in implementing and strengthening the WTO mandate for sanitary and phytosanitary measures, initially focusing most heavily on regulatory institution-building in the developing countries of the region, but with the United States and Canada also under pressure to rethink their zero tolerance approach for certain sensitive imports. Within NAFTA, substantial progress is being made to create a new regulatory regime in Mexico, converting what was formerly a highly discretionary import licensing procedure into a system of prior notification, transparency, and harmonized standards. Specific issues being addressed within NAFTA include the harmonization of pesticide tolerance standards between the United States and Canada, modification of Mexican certification for U.S. sweet cherry imports, and a relaxation of the U.S. "zero tolerance" ban on imports of Mexican avocados.

The FTAA Working Group on Sanitary and Phytosanitary Measures also links its work closely to the Uruguay Round-WTO agreement, again with eight specific references in its March 1996 report, and most of its recommendations follow the pattern of accelerating the implementation of WTO guidelines: create an inventory of all agreements on sanitary and phytosanitary measures in the Hemisphere; recommend specific ways to enhance transparency and information sharing; identify and make recommendations for practices that need improvement; promote understanding of the WTO agreement through training and other technical assistance; develop standards for harmonization of accreditation and certification services; and work toward common approaches for risk assessment. The final section of the March 1996 working group report, however, goes a step further in calling for a distinct regional system "that will permit the implementation *and broadening* of the WTO-SPS agreement" (emphasis added). An organizational chart is added for the "SFM Hemispheric Sub-System (FTAA),"[6] which will permit "the adoption of common positions in international forums."

These initial actions by the FTAA working group will undoubtedly help regulatory institution-building for developing countries within the Western Hemisphere, but it is not clear to what extent a more transparent and scientifically based system (including the application of something greater than zero risk assessment) will open trade to longstanding unreasonably restricted markets. Chile remains wedded to a zero risk mentality, and farmers came out in the streets to protest association with Mercosur that threatened the protection of Chile's environment. Mercosur is attempting to harmonize sanitary and phytosanitary standards on an apparently more restrictive basis, viewed in Washington with some concern as potentially threatening to U.S. farm exports. In parallel, however, U.S. consideration of the "regionalization rule" for risk assessment, which, for example, would permit beef exports to the United States from regions of Argentina untainted by hoof-and-mouth disease, presents the basis for mutual market-opening negotiations within a new system more firmly based on scientific principles. What is beyond question is that sanitary and phytosanitary regulatory regimes are of considerable importance to market access in the agricultural sector, and that NAFTA/FTAA, building on the Uruguay Round agreement, is breaking new ground toward a more open and scientifically based regulatory system in the Western Hemisphere.

Policy Area 5: Subsidies, Antidumping, and Countervailing Duties

Policy area 5 comprises three distinct issues—agricultural subsidies, nonagricultural subsidies, and antidumping—each with a distinct Uruguay Round outcome and NAFTA/FTAA role. The common element is their almost total immersion in national regulatory regimes. The Uruguay Round agreement achieved a breakthrough for reducing agricultural subsidies, including 20–36 percent cuts in export subsidies and domestic support programs over five years, after which a further liberalization of agricultural trade will be negotiated within the WTO. The Uruguay Round agreement on subsidies for nonagricultural trade also produced a significant result by more clearly defining limits on domestic subsidies affecting trade, subject to the strengthened WTO dispute settlement mechanism. In contrast, the Uruguay Round agreement for antidumping, after several years of intensive negotiation, resulted in little effective change from the existing GATT provisions, and U.S. implementing legislation made regulatory practices in the United States even more protectionist than before. In parallel, antidumping import restrictions are proliferating as developing countries adopt laws and regulations modeled on those in the United States and the EU.

All three of these issues are addressed in the NAFTA/FTAA regional context, and two of them—agricultural subsidies and antidumping—could produce results with far-reaching impact on the multilateral trading system. Agricultural export subsidies were largely eliminated within NAFTA, although this elimination was structured in terms of three separate agreements—continuation of the existing U.S.-Canada agreement and new bilateral agreements for U.S.-Mexican and Mexican-Canadian agricultural trade. The U.S.-Mexico agreement, phased in over fifteen years, calls for almost total elimination of border restrictions on trade, while U.S.-Canadian agricultural trade has more broad-based exceptions. The FTAA working group began by requesting preparation of an "Inventory of Agricultural Export Subsidies and Other Measures of Similar Commercial Effect" within the Hemisphere as well as a report on "European Subsidized Agricultural Exports to the Americas." Many issues of regulation are involved, including the fact that only a limited number of countries in the Hemisphere currently provide notification on the use of agricultural subsidies. The big question, however, is whether the FTAA will include free trade, or something close to it, for the agricultural sector, and the working group is considering proposals from member governments aimed at the eventual elimination of all trade distorting export practices affecting agricultural exports within the Hemisphere. Such an outcome would have various regulatory implications, including the possible use of countervailing duties for subsidized imports entering the FTAA from third countries, as well as the impact on future multilateral negotiations in the WTO, particularly between the EU and the Western Hemisphere grouping. A February 1997 draft report by the working group broached some of these issues by posing an approach whereby FTAA members would commit not to use export subsidies for certain farm goods, combined with a request that, "all external supplying countries refrain from the use of export subsidies when exporting to the Hemisphere.[7]

The principal significance of NAFTA for nonagricultural subsidies and the use of countervailing duties as a "trade remedy" is the special procedure for dispute settlement under Chapter 19, whereby binding dispute panel decisions substitute for national judicial review with respect to the application of countervailing duties and antidumping laws. This procedure has the immediate advantage of reducing the time for dispute settlement to a maximum of eighteen months under NAFTA compared with up to five years in national courts. The NAFTA dispute procedure also has advantages over the WTO mechanism in that panel decisions go into effect automatically, and restitution with interest is made for previously deposited duties. There are relatively few subsidies/countervailing disputes within NAFTA, although the major problem of Canadian lumber exports to the United States illustrates the advantages and disadvantages of the NAFTA regulatory framework. Canada first challenged the U.S. imposition of countervailing duties on its lumber exports within NAFTA and won its case under Chapter 19 procedures, receiving over $800 million in restitution payments. Then the United States simply changed its law in blatant violation of WTO commitments, but under NAFTA this is not relevant, so Canada would have had to take its case to the WTO. Canada finally settled out of court through a negotiated bilateral export quota. The FTAA working group is compiling basic information on subsidies and countervailing duty procedures throughout the Hemisphere and is considering technical training for officials responsible for such laws, but with a relatively low priority based on the 1996 working group finding that "antidumping is the most frequently used form of trade remedies; countervailing duties have been applied to a lesser degree and only by three countries in the region."

Antidumping is thus a far more important challenge in this policy area for NAFTA/FTAA, as it is for the WTO. The NAFTA result thus far centers on Chapter 19 dispute resolution, and most cases have been resolved promptly by unanimous panel decision. This procedure, however, as described above for the Canadian lumber countervailing duty dispute, is based solely on the application of existing laws within NAFTA members, even when the law is contrary to WTO commitments—laws which, as long applied in the United States and Canada and increasingly so in Mexico, produce highly trade-distorting results. Regulatory procedures for determining export price and assessing injury can defy economic reason, and the large administrative costs and unpredictable delays involved can in themselves eliminate small- and medium-size exporters from the market. A prominent antidumping abuse within NAFTA by the United States in 1996 was the threat of antidumping sanctions on imports of Mexican tomatoes, motivated by domestic political pressures during a presidential election year rather than any convincing evidence of dumping, which led to Mexico accepting "voluntary" export quotas. It can only be hoped that this is the rare exception and not the rule.

The broader question for NAFTA/FTAA therefore is whether a more far-reaching solution to antidumping practices within a free trade area can be achieved which would constrain if not eliminate antidumping sanctions. They were eliminated in the European Common Market and, in 1988, within the Australia-New Zealand free trade arrangement on the grounds that competition policies within the free trade area were unified or sufficiently compatible and that dumped products, within a free trade area, can be dumped back into the exporting country market, as they can among states or provinces within national economies. During negotiation of the U.S.-Canada free trade agreement, the issue of a phaseout of antidumping sanctions was raised, but shunted aside for future review, and a similar result occurred during NAFTA negotiations when the United States was even more opposed to any relaxation in antidumping procedures. The outlook for basic change in the policy framework for antidumping now appears even bleaker as Mexico applies antidumping to the satisfaction of its domestic industries, including the controversial criterion of anticircumvention. The FTAA working group is likewise more restrained in its mandate for antidumping compared with the free trade objective in agriculture, and is limited to considering proposals "for *improving* rules and procedures governing the operation and application of trade remedy laws" (emphasis added). No mention is made of a possible phaseout. One interesting development in the other direction is the exclusion of antidumping procedures as a trade remedy in the Canada-Chile free trade agreement concluded in November 1996. Within Mercosur, antidumping is not explicitly addressed, but it could be eliminated as the customs union is implemented, which would pose a problem of dual standards within the FTAA. Meanwhile antidumping sanctions proliferate throughout the Hemisphere.

The challenge of reducing or eliminating the trade-distorting effects of antidumping regulations should not, however, be abandoned. Progress could more easily be achieved within a regional free trade agreement, for reasons noted above, than on a global basis in the WTO. The outcome will be determined by political constituencies within member countries, and principally among private sector interests. Now that Mexico and Canada bring more antidumping complaints against U.S. exporters than vice versa, U.S. export industries should become more interested in a mutual rollback. Similarly, export-oriented industries throughout the Hemisphere should be considering the cost advantages of more restricted use if not an end to antidumping procedures among FTAA members. The U.S. steel industry has long been the dominant political force for ever more restrictive U.S. antidumping practices, but even this industry is becoming somewhat more competitive internationally. Lower cost "mini" mills are becoming larger, with "mini" Nucor soon to become the second largest U.S. steel producer, and with a CEO who has opposed antidumping practices. One approach for phasing out antidumping within NAFTA/FTAA would be to proceed on a sector-by-sector trial basis as the free trade agreement is implemented, perhaps leaving steel for last. The antidumping challenge, moreover, needs to be considered in an integrated way with competition policy, discussed below under policy area 9.

Policy Area 6: Government Procurement

Government procurement practices throughout the world are undergoing fundamental change as public enterprises are subject to more stringent standards of commercial viability, deregulation, and various stages of privatization. The scope of international competition is likewise broadening, with enormous trade-creating potential on the order of tens if not hundreds of billions of dollars per year. The entire process of public procurement liberalization, however, is enmeshed with regulatory regimes at the national, provincial, and local levels, including wideranging special provisions such as for national security exceptions and small business set-asides. In this dynamic context, the Uruguay Round achieved a substantial increase of WTO market access commitments for government procurement while NAFTA produced a breakthrough in terms of industrialized/developing country relationships.

The Uruguay Round agreement expanded the scope of the existing GATT government procurement code to cover state and provincial governments and services contracts. The annual value of procurement subject to international competition was also increased to about $400 billion, of which the United States and the EU accounted for a little over $100 billion each. Two major shortcomings, however, remain with the WTO agreement. First, market access is limited to specified sectors and projects, with everything else excluded. And second, participation in the government procurement agreement, unlike almost all other parts of the Uruguay Round agreement, is voluntary, and membership remains limited to the industrialized countries, with South Korea the only new signatory during the Uruguay Round. As a consequence, the agreement is on a "conditional MFN" basis, with market access commitments limited to signatory members. Post–Uruguay Round, a working party on greater transparency in government procurement was established at the 1996 Singapore meeting, directed largely at corrupt practices, but which could eventually lead to broader participation in the WTO government procurement agreement.

NAFTA achieved major advances with respect to both shortcomings of the WTO government procurement agreement. It is "principle-based," in that all procurement is open except for listed exceptions. Broad sectors remain excepted, but Mexico did open its state electric power monopoly, state petroleum industry, and wide-ranging construction contracts to bidding by NAFTA member companies. The United States, in turn, lifted its Buy America provisions for Mexican firms (as it had earlier for Canada in the U.S.-Canada free trade agreement). NAFTA commitments do not, however, apply at the state and provincial levels. The implementation process for NAFTA, moreover, involves intensive institution-building, particularly in Mexico, to ensure open and competitive bidding for government procurement contracts, which is proceeding on a constructive basis. A learning process has begun in the private sectors of member countries, with joint venture bidding proving to be a convenient approach for initial contract bids. Consultations between governments are underway to improve and extend the agreement over time, including such issues as application at the state and local levels of government, national set-asides, technical assistance for small businesses, and the extension of electronic transmission of sellers under U.S. procurement practices to Mexican and Canadian firms.

FTAA preparations for government procurement began later than for the other groups discussed thus far, with the creation of a working group at the March 1996 Cartagena meeting. The mandate for this working group—as for the remaining three working groups presented below—is also briefer, with the first step a compilation of existing laws and regulations in participating countries and the final task, common to all four working groups, to make "specific recommendations on how to proceed in the construction of the FTAA in this area." Extension of a government procurement agreement similar to that in NAFTA throughout the Hemisphere would, of course, be very significant in bringing a large grouping of developing countries into this area of commitments and setting the stage for a later broadening of participation in the WTO agreement. Mexican post-NAFTA free trade agreements with Colombia, Venezuela, Costa Rica, and Bolivia all include government procurement provisions modeled on NAFTA, which sets a precedent in this direction for the FTAA. The FTAA objective for Mercosur countries, however, is not yet clear.

Policy Area 7: Intellectual Property Rights

The Uruguay Round agreement brought intellectual property rights (IPRs) within the WTO mandate, including the national treatment principle, a basic set of standards for protecting intellectual property, enforcement obligations, and recourse to the WTO dispute settlement mechanism. NAFTA locked in Mexican laws with even higher standards for the protection of intellectual property, including the elimination of compulsory licensing in the pharmaceutical sector and protection of certain "pipeline" products. The biggest difference between the two agreements, however, is in their schedules of implementation, with the Uruguay Round providing developing countries generally five years and up to thirteen years for the pharmaceutical sector to implement the IPR provisions, while NAFTA gave Mexico only one year from the time the agreement came into effect in 1995.

Enforcement of IPR agreements at all levels—multilateral, regional, and bilateral (as in the case of the U.S.-China agreement)—is proving to be extraordinarily complex and contentious, and with the leisurely pace of WTO implementation, NAFTA becomes an important precedent for adaptation of legal and regulatory frameworks in a major developing country. The United States and Mexico have established a regularly meeting bilateral working group on intellectual property rights to address IPR enforcement, including inadequacies in Mexican law enforcement procedures. For example, while NAFTA requires that Mexico adopt procedures to allow U.S. rights holders to request Mexican customs authorities to suspend the release of goods with counterfeit trademarks or pirated copyright goods, in 1996 it was still not clear whether the customs authorities or other agencies or the courts were empowered to issue orders for such suspension. In general, enforcement measures are on the rise in Mexico, with 343 raids during 1995 in response to complaints by the U.S. recording industry, but court prosecutions are much slower in materializing.

Within the FTAA, IPRs will be a contentious area of negotiation for establishing standards. Mercosur countries indicate they are not prepared to go beyond Uruguay Round commitments while NAFTA members will presumably press for the higher NAFTA standards. The United States designated Argentina as one of only nine trading partners globally in its 1996 "priority" list for aggressive enforcement of IPRs under the infamous "special 301" authority, and ten out of twenty-six trading partners on the lower category "watch list" are also in the Western Hemisphere. At a minimum, compulsory licensing and other problem issues in the pharmaceutical sector will have to be resolved between the United States and Argentina during the course of FTAA negotiations.

Overall, however, the enforcement dimension of IPRs within an FTAA will likely have a more important impact on trade than will a further raising of standards, and this enforcement dimension consists of a comprehensive strengthening of regulatory regimes throughout the region to implement complex IPR standards and to suppress widespread counterfeiting and pirating of intellectual property. Counterfeit videos and CDs within the Americas, for example, are largely Asian imports involving border regulation and prosecution of elusive domestic vendors rather than the highly visible CD factories of notoriety in U.S.-China IPR disputes. The FTAA working group begins its work in this regulatory-heavy area with the tasks of recommending "methods to promote the understanding and effective implementation of the WTO agreement on trade-related aspects of intellectual property rights (TRIPs)," and identifying "possible areas for technical assistance, which countries may request, involving both the administration and enforcement of intellectual property rights.

Policy Area 8: Trade in Services

The Uruguay Round General Agreement on Trade in Services (GATS) establishes a framework of rules for trade in services, centered on an MFN commitment, with recourse to the WTO dispute settlement mechanism. There are also sectoral annexes for financial, telecommunications, air, and maritime services, as well as for movement of persons, which describe how the general rules and obligations apply in these sectors. The major shortcoming of the GATS is that the agreement does not, in fact, apply generally, but only to national schedules of market access commitments, which in the case of developing countries are very limited in scope in many cases. In addition, the MFN commitment does not yet generally apply to the important financial and maritime service sectors, pending negotiation of broader market access commitments in national schedules. The Uruguay Round agreement basically left liberalization of market access for trade in services for future negotiation, which is initially being played out in the two cited sectors, plus basic telecommunications for which an agreement was reached in 1997, including an MFN commitment.

The NAFTA agreement goes substantially beyond the Uruguay Round GATS both in terms of sectoral coverage and the process of liberalization of market access. It is truly a "general" agreement, covering all sectors except those specifically excluded, which are relatively few. Transitional schedules for liberalized access, particularly to the Mexican market, are included for financial, telecommunications, maritime, and air transport services, and these schedules have already been accelerated in the Mexican financial and value added telecommunications sectors. There have been some problems in implementation, particularly the U.S. delay in opening its market to Mexican trucks, but there is no question that services trade within North America is being opened on a free and comprehensive basis.

The outlook for the FTAA is especially unclear in this area in view of the wide difference in sectoral coverage between the GATS and NAFTA. Unlike the IPR situation for standards, however, it is not clear that Mercosur members will resist a broadening of coverage beyond what they included in the Uruguay Round agreement. Services are not explicitly addressed in the initial Mercosur agreement and are currently being developed in a separate protocol. The Mexican G-3 free trade agreement with Colombia and Venezuela is patterned on the NAFTA general applicability principle, but excluded sectors have still not been agreed upon and thus this part of the agreement is not yet in effect. One Uruguay Round-related aspect that could tilt the FTAA toward the comprehensive NAFTA model is that Article V of the GATS requires a regional free trade agreement which covers services to include "substantial sectoral coverage" (similar to the "substantially all the trade" provision of GATT Article XXIV for goods).

In any event, the degree of inclusion of trade in services within an FTAA will have a major impact on the economic result. The financial, telecommunications, and transportation sectors constitute the basic infrastructure for trade in increasingly information-based economies, and these sectors have traditionally been highly protected and inefficient throughout Latin America. These sectors are also going through a transformation within most Hemispheric nations, in the direction of deregulation, privatization, and enhanced competition, a process deeply enmeshed in often antiquated national regulatory regimes and legal frameworks. The interaction between NAFTA-induced modernization of the Mexican regulatory/legal framework for the services sector, based on free trade, and parallel developments elsewhere in the region—particularly within Mercosur countries—will likely shape the course of FTAA negotiations in this area.

Policy Area 9: Competition Policy

Competition policy was not part of the Uruguay Round agreement or NAFTA, which makes its selection as one of the designated policy areas for FTAA preparations unique. Competition policy is also on the post–Uruguay Round work programs for various other trade policy bodies, including the WTO, the OECD, and APEC, but again the FTAA initiative is unique in that its anticipated schedule for prenegotiation preparations and actual negotiations puts it at the forefront, in a path-breaking position to deal with yet another area of national legal and regulatory systems.

Competition policy is especially elusive as a subject for international negotiation because of the lack of clear definition, or more precisely the wide range of possible definitions. There is a long history of attempts, dating back to those by the stillborn 1947 International Trade Organization (ITO) and including those by developing countries within the UN system over several decades, to focus on "restrictive business practices" and other suspect activities of multinational corporations. The United States has more recently pursued a narrowly defined set of antitrust policy objectives related to market access for U.S. exports in bilateral talks with Japan and the EU. The EU, in turn, has a broad-based common competition policy. There is also the important question, raised in policy area 5 above, as to whether a more harmonized international approach to competition policy should be addressed together with antidumping measures, since the latter are explicitly a "second-best" (and in reality something a lot worse) alternative to the lack of a sufficiently harmonized competition policy at the international level. The preliminary talks within the U.S.-Canada and NAFTA negotiations constitute a precedent for such a linkage in FTAA negotiations.

Competition policy also goes to the heart of the economic transformation underway since the mid-1980s in developing and former communist countries, centered on market-based reforms, deregulation, and privatization, which is especially active in the Western Hemisphere. Latin American economies were (and remain, to a large degree) hobbled by public and private sector monopolies, both highly protected from international competition, resulting in stagnant economic performance and related high levels of public corruption. The current trend toward privatization of public enterprises, in this context, poses the concomitant threat of simply converting a public monopoly into a private monopoly. The means to counter such a threat is an effective competition policy. Above all, competition policy limited to domestic firms is becoming less and less relevant as national economies become more open and foreign investment/ trade dependent—the economic globalization phenomenon. Addressing competition policy in terms of international as well as national competition should be the starting point for the FTAA working group deliberations.

How the FTAA Working Group on Competition Policy will proceed remains to be seen, but it has had an active initial stage. The March 1996 mandate is brief, mainly fact-finding about existing policies and practices, which should in itself be revealing in terms of legal and regulatory frameworks, ranging from the highly litigious U.S. system to the amorphous to nonexisting systems in many of the small and least-developed economies in the region. Only about ten Latin American countries currently have functioning competition policy regimes, and none has the 100 years of regulatory experience of the U.S. Federal Trade Commission and Department of Justice Anti-Trust Division. Bridging the North/South divide in regulatory regimes will thus face another important challenge in this area.

The working group got off to a quick and proactive start. At their first meeting, in May 1996, initial discussion indicated interest in a broad scope of inquiry, including antitrust, intellectual property rights and antidumping policies. A follow-up, week-long seminar in August addressed the subject "Competition Policies and the Economic Reform Process in Latin America," and several additional meetings produced wide-ranging though inconclusive results.

The momentum in South America for addressing competition policy in the context of economic reforms, including trade liberalization, has grown rapidly in the 1990s. Active government interest has developed in Brazil, Chile, Mexico, Peru, Venezuela, and most recently Argentina. Mercosur has a working group on competition policy, but it has not yet produced results. The challenge for the FTAA working group is to convert this interest into actions to build effective and more harmonized competition policies throughout the region, including the necessary regulatory mechanisms for implementation.

Mutually Reinforcing Regulatory Regimes: Conclusions

The foregoing discussion presents a wide range of trade-related policies which are broadening and strengthening regulatory regimes within the Western Hemisphere. Other policy areas will undoubtedly be drawn in as the FTAA initiative goes forward. For example, Western Hemisphere finance ministers met in New Orleans in May 1996 and created a Working Group on National Financial Markets Regulations to examine existing financial regulations as a step toward harmonization. The Inter-American Development Bank (IDB) was asked to create a bank supervisor training institute and to study standardization goals, while the finance ministers agreed to meet again within two years with the hope of institutionalizing such gatherings, possibly linked to the FTAA. Environmental and labor standards might also be brought within the FTAA, although these issues are bogged down by partisan disagreement in the United States—with Republicans opposed to their inclusion in an FTAA—and by Latin American governments generally adverse to going beyond WTO decisions. Overall, however, there is no question that the dynamics of regional free trade are moving in the direction of more and more comprehensive policy commitments, with a consequent increase in pressures toward harmonization of regulatory regimes. The net assessment of this harmonization process to date for NAFTA implementation and FTAA preparations can be summarized in terms of three dimensions:

1. Institution-Building. This is the most clear cut, unambiguous aspect of regulatory regime development on a mutually reinforcing basis between NAFTA/FTAA and the WTO. It is difficult to overemphasize the importance and complexity of building modern regulatory—and legal—systems in support of open trade and investment. The task has a heavy developing country orientation, and indeed the level of regulatory regime development is a key indicator of the overall level of industrialization and modernization within a national economy. In more negative terms, the lack of a clearly defined, transparent, and well-administered regulatory regime is a likely indicator of a high level of public corruption, endemic in many developing country trading systems. Mexico clearly understands these indicators and is acting forcefully, in close collaboration with its

NAFTA partners, to create a modern regulatory system. The FTAA working groups, likewise, are engaged in a learning process that could produce tangible results well before an FTAA is reached. Moreover, both NAFTA and FTAA regulatory institution-building are consistently supportive of WTO implementation of the Uruguay Round agreement, as evident throughout the nine policy areas examined above.

2. Substantive Scope. The nine policy areas also demonstrate how NAFTA/FTAA regional integration is broadening the substantive scope of more harmonized regulatory regimes, which reinforce the existing WTO mandate and serve as a leading edge for developing the future WTO work program as well as free trade initiatives elsewhere, such as in APEC. Examples of broadened scopes for the existing WTO mandate include trade in services, government procurement, standards, and sanitary and phytosanitary measures. Examples of leading-edge policy areas are investment and competition policies. As in the case of institution-building, the developing country relationship is central in all of these areas of broadened policy scope. The stronger, more harmonized a regulatory regime is when adopted in the Western Hemisphere, the more likely and easily it will become an extension to the WTO. There are, however, potential conflicts as well in establishing the scope of regulatory regimes. Within the Western Hemisphere, differences are likely to develop between NAFTA and Mercosur members with respect to the strengthening of IPR standards and sectoral coverage for trade in services. Multilaterally, the course of negotiation on rules of origin criteria within the FTAA initiative could have adverse consequence for the WTO mandate in this area.

3. Trade Liberalizing Impact. This is the least clear of the three effects and a matter of some debate among economists, but on the whole, Western Hemisphere free trade should be strongly positive in terms of trade creation and economic growth. Traditional analysis of trade-creating versus trade-diverting effects when a free trade agreement is formed demonstrates that the more broad-based and comprehensive a free trade area is, the more likely the trade-creating will outweigh the trade-diverting effects. This is clearly the situation within NAFTA, and even more so within an FTAA, where both the country and policy coverage are very broad. Moreover, such traditional analysis is based on the "static" effects of free trade from changes in relative prices directly resulting from the elimination of import barriers. More recent assessments of the "dynamic" growth effects of free trade indicate additional trade-creating effects, possibly several times larger than the static gains, especially in developing countries. In this context, the process of building modern regulatory regimes can contribute significantly to reaping the dynamic gains from trade. An FTAA, finally, as with NAFTA, would not generally raise barriers to third countries, and could result in a locking in of unilaterally reduced barriers implemented throughout Latin America in recent years but not yet bound within the WTO. There are, however, some exceptions to this assessment. Mercosur has been criticized for permitting increased protection against nonmembers, particularly in the Brazilian automotive sector, and an FTAA would have to resist any such increases in border restrictions. Other possible exceptions concern transitional quota restrictions in the textiles and agricultural sectors, as well as the rules of origin issue. These latter problem areas—which are deeply regulatory in character—will be important for defining the future FTAA/WTO relationship, and will require statesmanship and strong leadership on the part of Western Hemisphere leaders.

The issue of leadership for achieving free trade in the Western Hemisphere is, in fact, far more critical than the need for political will to address specific problem issues. Leadership needs to be broad-based throughout the Hemisphere, including large and small countries. The absence of key elements of leadership have cast a dark cloud over prospects for an FTAA. Of particular concern have been the shortcomings of U.S. trade policy leadership during 1995–97, which received widespread criticism. Clearly a strong U.S. trade policy leadership role, with firm bipartisan support, needs to be reestablished if an FTAA is to become reality. The outlook for 1998 and beyond is more hopeful. Mexico has weathered the financial crisis of 1995, which, although unrelated to NAFTA, was used to attack further free trade agreements by NAFTA critics. The three-year report card for NAFTA, indeed, is generally positive, which should bolster support to move ahead with an FTAA.[8]

There remain, however, two noteworthy elements of leadership that will likely be decisive for a successful FTAA. The first is a proactive U.S.-Brazilian collaboration. As indicated in most of the policy areas, final agreement will center on the NAFTA/Mercosur relationship, and within Mercosur Brazilian leadership is key. The critical test will not be the technical issues of harmonized regulatory regimes which, as explained in the foregoing

section, are for the most part compatible among FTAA participants, but rather the political will of the United States and Brazil
to follow through and negotiate a comprehensive regional free
trade agreement. The prospect for such U.S.-Brazilian collaboration elicits skeptical reactions from trade policy experts, and the
Uruguay Round experience was not encouraging, but initial interaction within the FTAA framework has been somewhat more
promising.

The other element of leadership, which is even less clearly
engaged, but which is of special importance for progress on the
many regulatory/legal issues addressed in this essay, is that of
the private sector. Since the early 1980s, private sector leaders
have been out in front of governments in developing liberal
trade initiatives, at the multilateral and regional levels. This
was generally the case during the Uruguay Round, and it has
carried over to APEC, the OECD investment policy negotiations, and the launching of the FTAA initiative at the Miami
summit meeting in December 1994. Such private sector leadership has evolved from a predominant U.S. orientation to a balanced North America/European/Japanese relationship, and is
also developing steadily within the Asia-Pacific region. It is less
advanced, however, within the Western Hemisphere. Private
sector participation at the FTAA ministerial meetings has been
limited and uneven, and for some countries private sector repre-
sentatives are picked by governments as informal spokesmen
for official views rather than as forward thinking advisors on
new free trade objectives. The twelve FTAA working groups are
thus far composed solely of government officials, with technical
support coming from the international secretariats of the OAS,
the IDB, and the UN Economic Commission for Latin America.
However, for issues ranging from intellectual property rights to
financial services to industrial standards to competition policy,
the views and expertise of the private sector will be essential
input, sooner or later, and the sooner the better.

If the leadership is forthcoming along these lines—from the
United States, Brazil, other governments, and the private sector—the FTAA, in conjunction with NAFTA implementation,
will emerge to play an important role in the further development of the global trading system. At a minimum, the building
of modern, effective regulatory regimes in more than thirty
developing countries in the Western Hemisphere will be central
to this role, a vital institution-building process greatly supportive to the post–Uruguay Round WTO mandate at the multilateral level.

The relationship of NAFTA/FTAA to broader questions of an extended policy scope for the trading system and the further reduction of trade barriers, including the interaction of the multilateral WTO with the principal regional free trade groupings that are evolving in Europe, the Western Hemisphere, and across the Pacific, are addressed in detail in essay 6, but are summarized here with respect to NAFTA/FTAA in terms of three concluding observations:

1. The NAFTA/FTAA process is almost entirely supportive of a strengthening and broadening of the WTO multilateral system. Broader market access commitments by Western Hemisphere developing countries for trade in services and government procurement and new commitments in the areas of investment policy and reduced agricultural subsidies should all be supportive of moving the WTO in these liberal trade directions as well. More far-reaching challenges within FTAA negotiations include developing more rational policy frameworks for rules of origin and the antidumping/competition policy relationship, although at this point the likelihood of this happening is very low.

2. The NAFTA/FTAA process is out in front of the APEC free trade objectives in terms of target dates and prenegotiation preparations within the FTAA working groups. The important overlap in membership of the United States, Canada, Mexico, and Chile, however, provides the opportunity for stimulating a transfer of progress from the Western Hemisphere across the Pacific and into the APEC framework. A more serious effort on the part of APEC to negotiate an investment agreement is one potential target, as well as broader market-access commitments for financial, telecommunications, and transportation services.

3. The NAFTA/FTAA relationship with Europe is currently very limited with respect to the integration of regulatory regimes, but it could be the most important of all for the ultimate integration of the WTO multilateral system with the major regional free trade groupings. The trigger would be some form of transatlantic free trade agreement (TAFTA), as described in essay 3. The New Transatlantic Agenda has strong private sector participation and is already deeply engaged in many of the regulatory issues addressed in the FTAA working groups. If this action program should move forward over the next couple of years to discussion of a transatlantic free trade agreement, it would proceed within the same timeframe as the FTAA negotiations, and the two would have to be assimilated in some way in view of the critical North American participation in both. A

TAFTA initiative should, in fact, have a salutory effect on harmonizing regulatory regimes both within the Western Hemisphere and across the Atlantic since parallel discussions already underway about free trade between the EU and Mexico and Mercosur could be folded within a broader European-Western Hemisphere design. At that point, the overarching trade strategy question could no longer be avoided as to how the multilateral and regional systems—including regulatory regimes—can best be amalgamated.

5

APEC and the Interregional Triad

The world economy has had a tripolar orientation since the 1960s, with industrial development, trade, and international investment concentrated in Western Europe, North America, and East Asia. This concentration strengthened substantially during the 1980s, and by 1990, half of world trade took place within the three regions and another quarter among them, while the relative shares of foreign direct investment were even higher. These market shares appear to have leveled off or declined slightly in the 1990s, but the tripolar relationship continues to dominate the global economy.

The evolution of the world trading system has reinforced this tripolar economic orientation. Multilateral trade liberalization within the GATT has been undertaken principally by the industrialized countries, while regional free trade was adopted within Europe in the 1960s and within North American in the 1980s. Both of these regional free trade groupings—the EU and NAFTA—are currently in the process of broadening within Europe and the Americas. East Asia has not pursued the preferential free trade route, except for the ASEAN subregion, but has developed an extensive network of cooperative economic and financial relationships.

The net result is a world trade structure centered on three deepening intraregional relationships, posing the threat of splitting the world economy into two or three adversarial economic blocs. One way to help prevent a drift toward such regional blocs is to liberalize trade further on a multilateral basis within the WTO, as addressed at the Singapore ministerial meeting in December 1996. Another way is to build cooperative links among the three regional groupings. Such links have recently begun to form. The Asia-Pacific Economic Cooperation (APEC) was created in 1989, the New Transatlantic Agenda in 1995, and the Asia-Europe Meeting (ASEM) in 1996. Together they form a triad of interregional relationships that are very unequal in content at this point and face uncertain prospects over the next several years. In addition, and less-clearly understood but highlighted in this essay, there are significant interactions within the triad that are likely to intensify in the period ahead.

The most developed of the triad is APEC, and it is thus presented in greatest detail, first concerning its origins and then with respect to the ongoing quest for free trade within the transpacific region. The fledgling ASEM and New Atlantic Agenda are then assessed more briefly, and the concluding section brings together the three relationships in terms of an evolving interaction that could have important impact on the course of the international trading system, and, in particular, on the integration of the now separate multilateral and regional free trade tracks of the system.

APEC Origins

APEC was officially launched in Canberra, Australia, in November 1989, although the rationale and objectives for such a ministerial-level body were ill-defined at the outset. The Canberra meeting "demonstrated the value of closer regional consultations and economic cooperation on matters of mutual interest," based on "the impressive momentum of growth in recent years," but there were few specifics as to what this implied for APEC.[1] The only attempt at a common policy approach concerned efforts to bring the faltering Uruguay Round multilateral trade negotiations to a successful conclusion, and as for the impressive record of economic growth, no mention was made in the concluding statements regarding the private sector or the inherent linkages between private investment, trade, and economic growth, in part to avoid difficulties for later Chinese entry into APEC. Follow-on projects were limited to such noncontroversial technical areas as developing an improved database for regional trade and investment.

The political reasons underlying the Canberra initiative, however, received considerable attention and were to some extent conflicting. East Asians were alarmed about inwardly directed regional free trade in Europe and North America, and viewed APEC as a means for keeping the vital U.S. market open to Asian exports. Some Americans, in turn, were concerned about the possible formation of a Japan-centered East Asian trading bloc, while others considered more open trade across the Pacific a desirable goal in its own right. All APEC members viewed the Europeans as the principal roadblock to a successful Uruguay Round, and the formation of APEC posed an alternative regional approach if the multilateral GATT negotiations failed, in other words, an implicit threat to the Europeans.

The record of U.S. debate in the run-up to the Canberra meeting illustrates the conflicting U.S. views about the Asia-Pacific relationship, and free trade across the Pacific in particular. A 1988 study group, including senior officials and academics, produced *ASEAN-U.S. Initiative*, which recommended an ASEAN-U.S. free trade agreement as a long-term objective. A few individuals, including the American ambassador to Tokyo, Mike Mansfield, suggested serious consideration of a U.S.-Japan free trade agreement. As explained by one such lonely advocate: "A free trade agreement between the U.S. and Japan boggles the traditional, most-favored-nation mind. . . . Nevertheless, the idea is receiving persistent attention. . . . Some hard analysis within the U.S. government is clearly in order."[2] The preponderant official and expert view in Washington, however, was opposition to regional free trade across the Pacific unless the Uruguay Round failed. The prestigious Institute for International Economics (IIE) held a two-day conference on free trade areas and U.S. trade policy in November 1988, in which almost all the distinguished participants were negatively disposed to further regional free trade agreements by the United States—beyond the U.S.-Canada agreement—and the conference organizer, Jeffrey Schott of the IIE, in summarizing the main analytical conclusions and policy recommendations of the 400-page conference report, stated: "FTAs (i.e. free trade agreements) provide at best a third-best option for U.S. trade policy; consideration should be given to FTAs with countries in the Pacific Rim only if the GATT Round falters."[3] Fred Bergsten, director of the IIE and an active participant at the conference, was acknowledged to have provided "extensive and insightful comments" to the final report, which has a touch of irony as explained below.

In any event, APEC moved ahead slowly over the first few years, with the most significant development the entry of China, Taiwan, and Hong Kong as full and more or less equal members. Working groups were established for various areas of economic relationships, and close linkages developed with private sectors throughout the region through the APEC-based Pacific Business Forum. This was all positive, and the annual ministerial statements—including Chinese participation—of support for trade liberalization and for private sector investment-driven growth helped develop supportive political constituencies at home. An identity problem persisted, however, as to whether APEC would remain essentially a consultative body—like the OECD without the large secretariat—or become more action-oriented.

The breakthrough in defining APEC objectives came with the call by President Bill Clinton for a summit-level APEC meeting in Seattle in November 1993—referred to as a "leaders' meeting" to accommodate the three Chinese participants—which provided the political level impulse to develop a more specific set of commitments for the follow-on summit in Bogor, Indonesia, in November 1994. In Bogor, the leaders agreed to achieve free trade and investment in the region by 2010 for the industrialized members and by 2020 for developing country members. The current outlook for this APEC free trade objective is elaborated in the following section, but the sequence of events leading up to the momentous decision is recounted here first since it introduces a central theme of this essay, namely, that the recent course of inter- and intraregional trade relationships has not emerged from any grand design by governments, but rather from an interactive, dynamic process, with important unintended consequences.

The substantive preparations for the Seattle meeting focused on the report of an Eminent Persons Group (EPG) established the previous year and chaired by Fred Bergsten. The report laid out a "vision" for an Asia-Pacific Economic Community, including an "ultimate goal of free trade within the region." The leaders at Seattle were not prepared, however, to adopt free trade even as a dateless long-term goal, and the EPG was asked to develop their vision further for the subsequent Bogor meeting in November 1994. The EPG then pushed ahead to include dates for achieving free trade, and in August 1994 submitted its second report, with a final target date of 2020 and including a possible 2010 date for industrialized members. Private sector leaders, through the Pacific Business Forum, pressed for inclusion of the earlier 2010 date. Most APEC governments, including the U.S. and Japanese, nevertheless remained hesitant if not opposed to any free trade target date until shortly before the Bogor meeting, when Bergsten and his EPG colleagues briefed Indonesian President Suharto on their proposal, and Suharto endorsed the 2020 free trade objective with the earlier 2010 date for the industrialized countries. At this point, the

United States and Japan somewhat reluctantly joined in support, effectively backing into the far-reaching free trade commitment.[4]

The APEC Quest for Free Trade

Since 1994, APEC has retained political momentum through its annual leaders' meetings, supporting private investment and export-led growth and, in general terms, a progressive opening of markets. Specific results have been limited, but in some cases significant. A voluntary code on international investment policy was adopted in 1995, and a commitment was made at the November 1996 meeting at Subic Bay, Philippines, to negotiate an agreement in the WTO to substantially eliminate tariffs in the information technology sector by the year 2000. The objective of free trade in the region by 2010/2020, however, remains elusive, and there is widespread skepticism by outside observers about whether it will be achieved.

The first EPG report in 1993 correctly observed, with respect to a target date for achieving free trade, "a date without a specified work program and negotiating timetable might lack credibility and undermine rather than strengthen the process," and the lack of such a timetable continues to cast a cloud over the prospects for Asia-Pacific free trade. The 1995 Osaka Action Agenda called for "concerted unilateral actions" to reduce progressively barriers to trade and investment, but the individual action plans presented at Subic Bay in 1996, with a couple of exceptions, were very modest or vague. Two central questions remain unanswered concerning the definition of free trade and the relationship between the 2010 and the 2020 commitments.

As for the question of a free trade definition, APEC leaders speak of achieving free trade based on "open regionalism," but this benevolent-sounding term went undefined for years, and when the EPG attempted to define it in its 1994 report, the result was a series of options that had little explanatory content as to what would actually happen.[5] If the free trade arrangement is to be consistent with GATT/WTO commitments, which all APEC members insist will be the case, it must either be on a most-favored-nation (MFN) basis, in which case it might as well take place in the multilateral WTO framework in the first place, or on a preferential basis as provided for in GATT Article XXIV with respect to free trade agreements. The EPG definition says either approach is possible, although the preferential route would have to include an offer to nonmembers for reciprocal free trade, in other words, an open-ended preferential arrangement (also referred to as "conditional MFN"). APEC members, however, have still not stated which route they will be taking. Japan and other Asian countries are outspoken about avoiding the preferential route while stopping short of the obvious conclusion that this means free trade on an MFN basis. The United States, in contrast, appears to regard MFN free trade by 2010 as politically fatuous and thus implies support for the preferential route. A possible compromise approach would be selective bilateral free trade agreements under GATT Article XXIV, beginning with U.S., or NAFTA, agreements with Australia, New Zealand, and Singapore, but this would leave unresolved the preferential problem for East Asians and would be an admission that free trade would not be reached among all APEC members by the scheduled dates.

The second central question—the interrelationship between the 2010 and 2020 commitments—has received less attention since it can appear to be well into the future while APEC members concentrate on their initial concerted unilateral steps. In fact, this question will have to be addressed over the next couple of years if the 2010 target is to retain credibility. The 2010 industrialized grouping will likely consist of the United States, Canada, Mexico, Japan, Australia, and New Zealand, and possibly South Korea, Chile, Taiwan, Singapore, and Hong Kong, leaving other ASEAN countries and China clearly in the 2020 developing country camp. The pressing importance of defining more precisely the 2010/2020 interrelationship can be illustrated most pointedly by considering the U.S.-China relationship. The most difficult action by far for the United States in achieving the APEC free trade goal would be to eliminate its generally high tariffs on textiles and apparel by 2010, which would be in conjunction with the phaseout of bilateral textile quotas, mostly against Asian exporters, by 2005, as part of the Uruguay Round agreement. This textile tariff elimination would almost certainly have to be phased over at least ten years and thus begin about 2001, which would, in turn, require President Clinton to seek approval from Congress a year or two earlier, or in the late 1990s. Congressional approval for eliminating textile and apparel tariffs will not be easy, to say the least, and will surely require clear commitments by China, among others, for across-the-board free trade, including nontariff restrictions such as import licensing and currency requirements. Based on the record of Chinese negotiations for initial WTO membership, this would require major further commitments by China over the next couple of years as well.

This summary presentation of the two central unanswered questions certainly puts a strong burden of proof on APEC believers to demonstrate how the 2010 target date will be achieved, but the presentation made here is strictly in terms of traditional Anglo-Saxon/GATT legal commitments for market access, including the concepts of reciprocity and the reduction of import barriers as a "concession" to be compensated. Asian participants in APEC, however, speak of a less formal Asian way which is not easily comprehended by the traditional Western mind, including that of the author. Asians in fact have been reducing some barriers to trade and investment on a unilateral and somewhat concerted basis. Singapore and Hong Kong eliminated their tariffs decades ago. Other ASEAN countries are reducing tariffs internally and externally on a more gradual, MFN basis, for example, with the still highly protected Philippines proclaiming that MFN tariffs—with limited exceptions—will reach a uniform level of 5 percent by 2004.[6] Japan already has very low nonagricultural tariffs, which it could—in uncharacteristically bold fashion—simply announce will be phased out by 2010 on an MFN basis. The greatest challenge, if the Asians are to move unilaterally to free trade with such alacrity, will be to prevent the Europeans from having a "free ride," that is, to keep Europeans from maintaining protection against Asian exports while Asia grants MFN free trade to European exports. And this, in turn, is how the conditional MFN card could become the key to the question of free trade definition posed above. Professor Ippei Yamazawa, the Japanese member of the EPG, presents the issue to the Europeans in typically subtle Asian form: "APEC should invite the EU to a joint initiation of a new round of global liberalization within the WTO. . . . APEC will surely interact closely with EU members in building the WTO. The new WTO regime will certainly be affected by the liberalization program that APEC adopts. Some suggest APEC should pressure the EU with discriminatory liberalization unless the EU accepts similar liberalization. But such a tit-for-tat approach may make the EU inward-looking and split the world economy into two groups. . . . If APEC and the EU take a joint

initiative in launching the new WTO round of multilateral liberalization, the free rider issue will be resolved, and the momentum for multilateral liberalization will increase immensely."[7]

In effect, Yamazawa is calling for a joint commitment to free
trade by APEC and the EU, within the WTO framework, which
Fred Bergsten, incidentally, proposed more forthrightly in his
May/June 1996 *Foreign Affairs* article, "Globalizing Free Trade"
(addressed more fully in essay 6). This is also a point of departure for assessing the potential significance of the ASEM.

The ASEM Potential Role

The first summit-level ASEM in Bangkok in March 1996—with
participation by members of the EU, Japan, South Korea, China,
and ASEAN—was heralded in much of East Asia as an important new international relationship, received a more muted
response in Europe, and went almost unnoticed in the United
States. ASEM remains undefined as anything more than a high-
level consultative mechanism, and its somewhat murky origins
contributed to the varied initial reactions.

The initiative for ASEM came from ASEAN leaders. Sin-
gaporean Prime Minister Goh Chok Tong publicly proposed the
first ASEM, while Malaysian Prime Minister Datuk Mahathir
Mohamad was believed to be a prime mover for the initiative.
Mahathir's deep reservations about APEC—he was the only
leader who refused to attend the first APEC leaders meeting in
Seattle—and his drive to create a separate East Asian grouping
apart from APEC, currently the East Asia Economic Caucus
(EAEC), led to the conclusion that one motive for creating
ASEM was to dilute, at least in relative terms, the preponderant
APEC relationship and perhaps thereby slow its momentum
toward free trade. The exclusion of Australia and New Zealand
from the initial ASEM in Bangkok, despite the strong desire of
these two countries to participate, added a racial dimension—
yellow/brown Asians meeting with white Europeans—and
thus a troubling political connotation.[8]

The self-evident mutual economic interest of Asian and
European leaders to meet on a regular basis was nevertheless
the overriding explanation for the creation of ASEM. The fact
that the transpacific economic relationship had developed so
quickly in structure and substance through APEC was reason

enough to establish a corresponding link between Europe and Asia—a triad interaction in the parlance of this essay. Europeans, in particular, were concerned about being left out of the burgeoning transpacific relationship and were more self-confident that they could compete in Asia as exporters and investors than they had been ten or even five years earlier. At the same time, however, the Europeans initially viewed the ASEM principally in terms of political-level consultations and were cautious at the preparatory stage not to have ASEM become too time-consuming a mechanism for distant travel by leaders and for committee and other support activities by staff. The U.S. lack of interest reflected the reality that ASEM would go forward no matter what Washington thought, and that it would probably remain benign, with little, if any, adverse effect on the course of APEC. The fact that ASEM added one more dimension to the growing network of regional trade relationships outside the multilateral WTO framework didn't appear to bother anyone, and the familiar pledge of allegiance to the multilateral trading system, a hallmark of regional trade groupings, was duly performed at Bangkok.

The congenial, informal exchange of views at the Bangkok meeting continues to characterize the ASEM process, and critics point to the lack of substantive commitments. Nevertheless, an organizational structure is taking shape, and a meeting-driven momentum is forcing political leaders to focus on more concrete objectives, similar to what happened at the early stages of APEC. At the foreign ministers meeting in Singapore in February 1997, the formulation of a "vision" group, analogous to the APEC EPG, was agreed upon, with a group draft report scheduled for the London ASEM summit in April 1998. Finance and commercial ministers, as well as lower-level groupings, met during the course of 1997.

ASEM, in any event, should not be overly discounted or ignored. It could come to play a significant role in the further evolution of the world trading system, but this will depend principally on what happens in the other two legs of the triad. As explained above, pressures within APEC to define its route to free trade could lead to an appeal to Europeans to join in a broader free trade initiative in the WTO, and initial soundings about such an initiative could be taken within ASEM. In other words, the East Asians could make a Yamazawa-like presentation within ASEM. This is unlikely at this point, however, because East Asians realize that the Europeans are not ready to respond positively to free trade with Asia. There is also a political/cultural obstacle for the diverse grouping of East Asians to come up with such a bold initiative—APEC/EU free trade—within the ASEM framework without the Americans in the lead or even present.

Rather, some further catalytic step would likely be necessary before the ASEM could be energized to play a more active, operational role, and such a step could well transpire in the third leg of the triad, the New Transatlantic Agenda, especially if this agenda should come to include serious consideration of a Transatlantic Free Trade Agreement (TAFTA). An indication of such a potential triad interaction comes from another Japanese observer, Noboru Hatakeyama, president of the Japan External Trade Organization (JETRO). In a presentation at the IIE in June 1996, Hatakeyama put forward, as "a personal idea," consultation between APEC and the EU, "to find out whether or not the EU is willing to implement similar liberalization plans" (i.e., free trade as is the objective within APEC). This would solve "the impasse between open regionalism and avoiding free riders by outsider economies." Hatakeyama up to this point tracks with the Yamazawa proposal, but he then goes a step further in explaining the benefits of such an "APEEC" (Asia-Pacific-Europe Economic Cooperation): "If APEEC is realized, the consultation process of TAFTA will be absorbed into APEEC, thereby possibly preventing NAFTA and the EU from formulating the world's largest FTA, and one which might discriminate against the rest of the world. . . . Frankly, I believe in the good conscience of leaders in NAFTA and the EU. If consultation is handled under the auspices of APEEC, they will not dare to formulate an unprecendently-large FTA that discriminates against the rest of the world and undermines the multilateralism of world trade."

Thus, what might happen across the Atlantic has already become a factor in the evolving APEC and ASEM relationships.

The New Transatlantic Agenda as a Catalyst

The United States is committed to free trade within the Western Hemisphere and across the Pacific with East Asia. The EU is broadening the European free trade grouping to the east and south to include over forty countries, and has offered to discuss free trade with Russia at some future point. The EU has also agreed to begin free trade discussions across the Atlantic with

Mexico and the South American Mercosur grouping. As a consequence, the United States and the EU have become conspicuous for not seeking free trade with one another.

This now could change through the New Transatlantic Agenda adopted at the U.S.-EU summit meeting in Madrid in December 1995. The economic section of the Agenda is broad in coverage but thin on specifics, with a pledge "to create a Transatlantic Marketplace by progressively reducing or eliminating barriers that hinder the flow of goods, services, and capital between us." A parallel private sector Transatlantic Business Dialogue was established with an agenda initially focused on closer coordination of regulatory policies. As with APEC and ASEM, the beginnings of this third leg of the triad are important for understanding the current outlook.

In early 1994, some European leaders began expressing interest in a Transatlantic Free Trade Agreement (TAFTA), and Canadian Prime Minister Jean Chrétien called for an EU/NAFTA free trade accord in the run-up to the G-7 summit in Halifax in July 1995. The reasons for interest in a NAFTA were partly economic, to reap the mutual benefits of free trade, and partly political/security to strengthen the faltering North Atlantic Alliance in the post–Cold War situation. The United States, however, was cool if not adverse to a TAFTA initiative. As noted earlier, in June 1995 when EU Commissioner Sir Leon Brittan proposed consideration of a TAFTA, Secretary of State Warren Christopher simply stated that the U.S. would give a TAFTA, as a possible long-term goal, "the serious study it deserves."

The outlook for the New Transatlantic Agenda is thus unclear, and on the surface at least, not encouraging with respect to a TAFTA. Little happened during 1996 and 1997 except for progress on several sectoral mutual recognition agreements. Nevertheless, the real test for the New Transatlantic Agenda, as explained in essay 3, is only beginning as the second Clinton Administration formulates a comprehensive trade strategy that includes the interaction of regional free trade initiatives moving forward within Europe, the Americas, and across the Pacific. What can be stated with respect to the triad relationship under review here is that once a serious U.S.-EU official dialogue on TAFTA were to get under way, and to the extent more political leaders on both sides of the Atlantic express positive interest, there will be a strong catalytic effect on both APEC and ASEM in terms of how Asia will react to the possible merging of the regional free trade groupings in Europe and North America. It will certainly encourage APEC leaders to be more focused on how they intend to achieve the free trade objective across the Pacific. The Hatakeyama concern will, in effect, rise high on the agendas of APEC and ASEM—triad interaction in full bloom.

Whither the Interacting Triad

The only certain conclusion that can be drawn from the foregoing discussion is that there currently exists a high degree of uncertainty as to how the three industrialized poles of the global economy—Western Europe, North America, and East Asia—will interact with one another in the period ahead. In terms of trade, all three are brought together most directly in the WTO, but momentum to broaden and deepen free trade within the regions and among the triad of interregional linkages, still in a fledgling state, will develop further in a complex, interactive way. Among the triad, APEC is the most clearly defined in terms of its objective for free trade and investment by 2010/2020, but it is at an impasse as to the path for achieving this goal. ASEM is least-developed and currently little more than a high-level consultative mechanism, but it could be energized by what happens in the other two parts of the triad relationship. The New Transatlantic Agenda, in turn, could play a catalytic role if the objective of creating a Transatlantic Marketplace takes the form of a TAFTA.

The term triad has been used here in its broad definition as a group of three closely related beings or things. The term also has a more precise musical meaning, however, as a chord consisting of three notes, or tones, which interact to a certain harmonic effect. For example, a major chord has a given tone or root, a major reassuring third, and a perfect fifth, while a minor chord has a root, a rather mournful minor third, and the perfect fifth. By analogy, the economic triad under discussion here currently has little harmonic content, although the APEC free trade objective sets the tone as the root to the other two relationships. If a TAFTA initiatives were forthcoming, this situation would move quickly to a minor chord sonority, with TAFTA becoming the perfect fifth and ASEM thrown into a minor mournful state. This, in turn, would leave open the possibility of ASEM developing further, based on dulcet Yamazawan themes, to achieve a triad of pleasantly conclusive major chord harmony.

6

From Here to Free Trade: The Quest for a Multilateral/Regional Synthesis

The first fifty years of the GATT/WTO multilateral trading system has been an extraordinary success story of reducing barriers to trade and stimulating economic growth throughout the world. During the 1980s, however, a fundamental restructuring of trade—and the trading system—began, which continues to gather momentum in the 1990s, and which requires, in turn, a fundamental rethinking of trade strategy.

There are many aspects of this changing structure of trade relationships which have received wide-ranging attention. Economic globalization is a central phenomenon, drawing national economies more closely together in terms of trade, international investment, and cross-border technology transfer. National companies are becoming more and more oriented to international markets. Governments are caught between political pressures to resist import competition and the imperative to more open trade policies in order to maintain a competitive position in world markets. On the whole, governments have pursued the trade-liberalizing route, thus reinforcing the overall globalization process. Moreover, trade liberalization has been proceeding at three levels—multilaterally through the Uruguay Round and the WTO, regionally through various free trade initiatives, and unilaterally as a matter of national self-interest by many developing countries and former and remaining communist countries.

This greatly changed, multifaceted context of trade relationships, compared with only a decade ago, presents a complex challenge for trade strategy formulation in the period ahead. Two critical developments in policy orientation, however, constitute points of departure for developing such a strategy, and will be decisive for the outcome.

The first critical development is that free trade, as distinct from progressive trade liberalization, has now become an explicit policy objective. This is most obvious in the proliferation of regional free trade initiatives underway in Europe, the

Americas, and across the Pacific, but it also emerged in the latter phase of the Uruguay Round through "zero-for-zero" tariff elimination by sector by the industrialized countries, which resulted in a more than doubling—from 20 percent to 44 percent—of the share of nonagricultural imports by these countries that will be free of duties on an MFN basis. Post–Uruguay Round, the industrialized and some newly industrialized countries continued this sectoral free trade approach through the 1997 Information Technology Agreement (ITA) to eliminate remaining tariffs in the information technology and telecommunications sectors, which would bring the duty-free share of industrialized country nonagricultural imports to about half. Initiative for such sectoral—as well as regional—free trade objectives comes largely from multinational corporations, who seek to rid themselves of border payments to governments and to achieve more predictable market access upon which to build internationally oriented investment and marketing strategies. Governments also find the free trade outcome easier to explain in terms of "reciprocity" in market access, subject to certain other things being equal, of which more below.

The second critical development is that while the multilateral trading system has been strengthened through the Uruguay Round agreement and the creation of the WTO, regional free trade agreements have the political momentum and are rapidly approaching parity with MFN commitments as the organizing principle for trade relationships. The EU is negotiating agreements in Eastern Europe and the Mediterranean basin which will lead to a free trade grouping of over forty countries. The intended FTAA will include another thirty-four countries, and the APEC free trade objective would add fourteen more. Thus, three-quarters of WTO members are committed to regional free trade between now and 2020. In trade terms, the share of global exports within free trade agreements will increase from about 45 percent today to 70 percent if all of the above objectives are achieved. In addition, a TAFTA, which would encompass another 7 percent of world exports, is under preliminary review, with significant political support on both sides of the Atlantic. The launching of formal talks toward such a transatlantic agreement would clearly tilt the balance of the trading system toward the regional free trade approach, of which much more below.

In view of these two developments—free trade as an explicit policy objective and the approaching parity between the multilateral MFN and regional free trade components of the overall trading system—the central question of trade strategy ahead is how to manage the interaction of these developments and to what end. Should multilateral and regional objectives continue to be pursued on largely separate tracks, or should they be integrated toward some common goal? If the latter, what role should free trade play, including the possible objective of multilateral free trade? And a key question often obscured or neglected, how should free trade be defined as an operational objective? In sum, the trade strategy challenge is to develop a multilateral/regional synthesis with particular focus on the uneven process underway toward free trade.

The following presentation addresses these strategic questions in terms of three basic scenarios for trade negotiations over the coming five to ten years. The first scenario is to pursue the current two-track course, basically a projection of official trade policy objectives, at the multilateral and regional levels. The second scenario is for a WTO free trade "Grand Bargain," to adopt the label of Fred Bergsten, who has put forward the most detailed proposal along these lines. The third scenario is for a multilateral/regional synthesis based on an extension and integration of regional free trade groupings, featuring a TAFTA initiative as the key catalytic step. This third scenario is judged to be the preferable approach for building a strengthened and truly multilateral trading system over the coming ten years, although at some cost to the concept of universality. It is clearly a more complex strategy to evaluate as well as to implement, and the final section of the essay thus elaborates broader U.S. foreign policy interests in such a strategy as well as the need for strong, concerted leadership, among the major industrialized countries in particular.

The Current Two-Track Approach

This scenario consists of the anticipated WTO action program at the multilateral level, while existing free trade objectives in Europe, the Americas, and the Asia-Pacific region move forward at the regional level on differing time schedules. In effect, the multilateral and regional trade liberalization tracks are pursued independently of one another, although within the vague concept of "gradual convergence" toward free trade at some undefined future point. The multilateral WTO track receives rhetorical priority, as expressed by WTO Director-General

Renato Ruggiero: "Maintaining the primacy of the WTO rules and dispute settlement system is vital, not as an end in itself, but in order to avoid a bedlam of competing and contradictory jurisdictions."[1] This multilateral track primacy, however, can be belied by actions at the regional level, and Europeans in particular appear disingenuous—pledging priority allegiance to the multilateral trading system while at the same time moving forcefully to create a preferential regional trading bloc among one-third of the WTO membership. Surely the intent of the forty-plus members of the anticipated European grouping is not to create a bedlam of competing and contradictory jurisdictions, but rather to assert the primacy of the European "acquis" over WTO rules and dispute settlement procedures.

Within this two-track scenario, the WTO action program will be important for consolidating and extending market-access commitments within the multilateral trading system. There is first the effective implementation of the Uruguay Round agreement. The greatly strengthened dispute settlement mechanism will be critically tested, and implementation of the complex and politically charged Uruguay Round commitments in the agriculture and textile sectors will require political courage, particularly by industrialized country governments. The post–Uruguay Round WTO action program, perhaps leading to a new round of multilateral negotiations, is based largely on the "built-in agenda" of commitments for further negotiations contained in the Uruguay Round agreement, in particular for the financial and basic telecommunications sectors in 1997, public procurement by 1999, and agriculture and services more generally by 2000. Possible new areas for negotiation, based on the ministerial declaration in Singapore in December 1996, include investment and competition policies, transparency in government procurement, and the trade-environment linkage. Overall, it is a very ambitious agenda.

One area of further trade liberalization within the WTO which remains vague is reduction or elimination of tariffs and related border restrictions such as quotas, import licenses, and currency restrictions, the traditional centerpiece of multilateral GATT negotiations and, of course, the core of regional free trade agreements. The conundrum facing the WTO in this area, post–Uruguay Round, is the great asymmetry between the industrialized countries and the newly industrialized "emerging market" countries in Asia, Latin America, and Central/Eastern Europe. Industrialized countries, as noted above, have eliminated or are in the process of eliminating tariffs, on an MFN basis, on half of their nonagricultural imports, and most remaining tariffs are either very low or in the textile sector and therefore subject to a rigidly negotiated ten-year Uruguay Round arrangement. The emerging market countries, in contrast, bound most of their tariffs in the Uruguay Round against future increase, but generally at very high levels of 20–40 percent or more, often well above actual rates. Moreover, quotas, import licensing requirements, and currency restrictions abound. This asymmetry in market access presents a major problem for any further "zero-for-zero" tariff elimination by industrialized countries, and was in fact a contentious issue within the pharmaceutical and other sectors in the final phase of the Uruguay Round, voiced as the problem of "free rider" benefits to the more advanced developing countries. The ITA includes limited participation by some developing countries, but not all. In any event, it is difficult to envisage how comprehensive reduction or elimination of tariffs and other border restrictions to trade can be negotiated within a WTO context of "reciprocity," whereby developing countries, contrary to all tradition and practice, would have to do far more rather than less import liberalization than would the industrialized countries.

A final issue of importance for the projected WTO action program is its leisurely pace. Negotiations in most cases would not begin for another two to three years, with a possible new round launched no sooner than 2000, and with concrete results not anticipated before 2005 at the earliest. The regional free trade track under this first scenario, in contrast, will likely proceed more rapidly and concretely, certainly in Europe and probably in the Americas, while in the process shifting the balance between the two tracks further toward comprehensive regional free trade relationships. Three aspects of this regional course stand out.

The first regional track aspect is the enormous significance of the broadening process of free trade within Europe. For four decades, regional free trade among EC and EFTA countries was a contained relationship, viewed as the exception to the MFN rule of the GATT multilateral system and an essential part of Western cohesion against the hostile Soviet bloc. Now, this limited grouping is expanding to the east and south with no clear limits. Ten countries in central and eastern Europe have in place or are negotiating free trade association agreements with the EU, as a stepping-stone to full membership, including the three

Baltic former Soviet republics. Turkey is engaged in negotiation of a customs union with the EU, and free trade agreements exist or are being negotiated with more than ten other Mediterranean Basin countries. This whole integration process has wide-ranging political as well as economic benefits, for the region and the global order, but it also changes in important ways member-state relationships, inside and outside of Europe, including within multilateral institutions. Within the WTO, for example, all forty-plus members of the European grouping will be obliged or tend to follow the unified position of the EU representative, and to cast forty-plus votes in decision-making, compared with one vote each for the United States and Japan.

The most far-reaching implication of the momentum for EU expansion to the east, however, is the evolving economic relationship with Russia and Ukraine. If political and economic reforms in these two countries muddle forward over the next several years, the compelling next step would be for them to apply for associate, free trade arrangements with the EU similar to those of the Baltic and Central European nations, and the EU would then be in a position of not being able to say no even if it wanted to. Western Europe is the natural market for Ukraine and European Russia, and the more and more apparent economic success of Poland and other Central European economies, based heavily on free access to the EU market, is the demonstration effect. The EU and Russia, in fact, have already agreed in principle to discuss a possible free trade agreement as early as 1998 if reforms go forward in Russia. Ukraine has even greater incentive for an early free trade agreement with the EU as a counter-balance to excessive economic dependence on Russia, and already is pursuing free trade with Central European countries. Such a European development, again, would have broad positive consequences, but at a cost to transatlantic solidarity with the United States. Even preliminary discussion of an EU-Russia free trade arrangement, whereby Russian exports to the EU would have preferential access compared with U.S. exports, would raise difficult questions in Washington, including the rationale for maintaining a troop presence in Western Europe against a perceived Russian threat. EU-Russian economic integration would also appeal to European nationalists, especially in Russia and France, as a means to consolidate a Europe from the Atlantic to the Urals and thus to regain status as a global power independent of the United States.

The second regional track aspect is what can be called the bridging of the North/South divide. In contrast with the asymmetric reciprocity conundrum within the WTO described above, regional free trade initiatives have been moving forward with little regard to the "special and differential treatment" for developing countries that pervades GATT/WTO tradition and practice. Mexico, for example, agreed within NAFTA to eliminate its much higher levels of import restrictions on a fully reciprocal basis with the United States and Canada, as in its self-interest, while at the same time in the Uruguay Round offering only modest tariff reductions and agreeing to bind many sensitive tariffs at 40 percent, or double the actual level. Similar reciprocal free trade agreements have been negotiated between the EU and the emerging market economies in Central Europe and are the basis for preliminary free trade discussions in the Americas and APEC, although in the latter case, at least, with a longer phase-in period for developing countries. It is difficult to overemphasize this distinction in institutional negotiating context between the GATT/WTO up to this point and what has been happening at the regional free trade level.

The third regional track aspect is the evolving definition of what is meant by a free trade agreement. At a minimum, it would mean the elimination of tariffs on nonagricultural imports, as well as closely related border restrictions such as quotas, import licensing requirements, and currency restrictions. Agriculture would have to be included to a large extent, if not completely. Trade in services, protection of intellectual property, subsidies, government procurement, and investment policies would also all likely be included in forthcoming free trade agreements, although most of these trade-related policies are only partially included, if at all, in the multilateral WTO. Such a "comprehensive" approach to free trade is vital to ensure that the elimination of border restrictions are not nullified or impaired, to use the famous GATT phrase, by other trade-related policies, and also to reflect the broadening interrelationships between trade in goods and services, investment, and technology transfers. Indeed, the term "trading system" has become misleadingly narrow in describing what is evolving in international economic relationships. The extension of regional agreements over the coming five to ten years, in fact, should help clarify this definition problem through the negotiated scope of "core agreements" as the basis for a free trade relationship.

Such core agreements would not be as comprehensive as the economic and monetary union relationship envisaged by the EU, and will probably be "plus or minus NAFTA" in scope.

In sum, this first scenario of two separate tracks has many positive elements for continuing the trade liberalizing process of past decades, mostly in the direction of gradual convergence, and could set the stage for a reappraisal five or ten years hence as to how to achieve a more definitive convergence between the multilateral and regional free trade dimensions of the overall trading system. There is a strong likelihood, however, that under this scenario, despite the ringing declarations at Singapore about the primacy of the multilateral system, regional groupings will strengthen and deepen their relationships at a faster pace than will the WTO multilateral structure, which could cause a disturbing drifting apart of Europe and North America, in particular, as well as growing concerns in Asia if the APEC free trade course does not produce early concrete results, which is also likely. It is therefore useful to consider alternative trade strategies to achieve a more definitive multilateral/regional synthesis during the coming five to ten year timeframe.

A WTO Grand Bargain

The simplest way to achieve convergence between the multilateral trading system and the various regional free trade agreements in place or in process would be to negotiate the elimination of remaining tariffs and other restrictions to trade on an MFN basis within the WTO. Such a multilateral free trade approach has been proposed from time to time over the years, most recently by Fred Bergsten, director of the Institute for International Economics in Washington: "There are enormous opportunities for further economic gain in eliminating remaining tariffs and non-tariff barriers. The Uruguay Round teed up these remnants of traditional protection for decisive action by converting all agricultural quotas into tariffs, phasing out quota protection for textiles and apparel, and binding most tariffs of developing countries. One last big push could condemn these practices to the dustbin of history."[2]

Bergsten terms his proposal a "Grand Bargain" between the industrialized and developing countries, whereby the former provide "insurance" that their markets will remain open, "including procedural safeguards against subtle methods of undoing prior market opening," and the latter offer free and full access to their more highly protected markets. Procedurally, agreement would be reached at a WTO trade summit meeting to achieve global free trade by 2010, "with a possible extension to 2015 or 2020 for the poorest nations."

The central question about the Grand Bargain proposal is whether it is politically feasible over this short- to medium-term timeframe, whereby the negotiation of global free trade would be inserted at an early date into the WTO action program, and indeed become its centerpiece. In terms of U.S. interests, almost all of the bargain would appear feasible, given strong presidential leadership, in keeping with broad bipartisan Congressional support obtained for trade-liberalizing initiatives in the past. U.S. tariffs are already generally very low, and much more would be gained for U.S. exports through free access to highly protected developing country markets. Global free trade in agriculture was the explicit and staunchly pursued U.S. objective in the Uruguay Round. In any event, the United States is already committed to free trade in the Americas and with East Asia, and, as explained below, political support for transatlantic free trade would be the easiest of all to obtain. The difficult issues for the United States would be such an early phaseout of textile and apparel tariffs and "more stringent multilateral disciplines" on antidumping duties, which Bergsten explicitly cites as one of the not-so-subtle methods of undoing prior market opening, but some arrangement for these issues could probably be negotiated if America's trading partners were to do their part of the bargain.

It is precisely the willingness of others to respond to the Grand Bargain proposal, however, that raises serious questions about its political feasibility, and which requires some greater specificity as to what an acceptable free trade agreement would need to encompass. Certainly all border restrictions on nonagricultural trade would have to be phased out. Agriculture would have to be included in a major way, although perhaps not completely in the initial phase. Investment policy is now clearly linked to trade in a growing number of bilateral and regional agreements, and would have to be part of the Grand Bargain. Intellectual property rights, trade in services, and government procurement, while all included in the Uruguay Round agreement, would require further commitments by developing countries. Competition policy, broadly defined, is also making its way into trade deliberations as an important dimension of overall market access relationships, and would certainly have to be part of an agreement that placed more stringent multilateral disciplines on antidumping duties. All of these trade and trade-related policies, in sum, would presumably have to be part of a WTO Grand Bargain, as they are, for example, in the NAFTA/ FTAA regional free trade context.

Whether the more advanced developing countries, in partic-ular, would be prepared to negotiate such a comprehensive free trade agreement for implementation by 2010, however, is extremely doubtful. Four examples of critical participants are sufficient to indicate that such a Grand Bargain is, at a mini-mum, premature:

1. India has undertaken market-oriented reforms over the past several years, but is far from freeing its imports of all tariffs and nontariff border restrictions. It objected to discussion of investment policy within the WTO until the eve of the Sin-gapore meeting and would almost certainly resist the Grand Bargain proposal in which it would have to take more far-reach-ing actions than almost any other major trading nation.

2. The ASEAN countries could be receptive in principle to a WTO free trade initiative as they were to the APEC regional free trade objective, but their performance to date regarding implementation is not encouraging. Some ASEAN members decry the U.S. trade policy approach of binding market-access commitments and highly legalistic rules and procedures, in favor of a more informal, flexible Asian approach, but the U.S. approach is what the GATT/WTO is all about. It is therefore highly doubtful that ASEAN countries would be any more forthcoming in the WTO than they have been up to this point in elaborating a specific plan and schedule for APEC free trade.

3. China has to be assumed to become a WTO member over the timeframe of the Grand Bargain proposal, which would become a mind-boggling challenge for quick integration into a comprehensive free trade relationship. The Chinese trading system is far from market-oriented in accordance with WTO precepts, and Chinese insistence on being admitted to the WTO as a developing country would not bode well for early accep-tance of free trade parity with the industrialized countries by 2010, as required by the Grand Bargain, or ten years earlier than the 2020 APEC target date.

4. Russia, too, can be expected to join the WTO over the next few years, but with a trading system still in a state of semi-development and uncertain decentralized control. A more modest association arrangement with the EU, as described in scenario one, is a more likely and practical next step for Russian convergence toward a longer-term free trade objective.

There are also major questions as to whether Europe and Latin America would be prepared to negotiate a free trade arrangement with East Asia. Longstanding concerns about unbridled import competition from Asia constitute at least one motive for these countries to maintain their free trade horizons at the regional level. Only the North American countries and Chile are committed to free trade with Japan, China, and other East Asian countries and, to some extent at least, the quiescence of the U.S. Congress and public about this commitment is due to its still-unspecified content.

There is finally the question of institutional capability for the newly established WTO to handle such a wide-ranging initiative. It took five years, beginning in 1981, to launch the GATT Uruguay Round, another eight years to negotiate an agreement, and a further ten years to implement it. WTO procedural complexities, based on the one-nation-one-vote principle, grow along with its burgeoning membership and remain to be tested within an organizational structure more rigid than prior GATT procedures. The establishment of WTO credibility as the multilateral foundation for the global trading system should not be threatened by overly ambitious objectives during its initial years of operation.

In conclusion, a WTO free trade Grand Bargain does not appear politically feasible at this time, although perhaps it will become so in ten years' time as the trading system evolves— and hopefully converges—further at both the multilateral and regional free trade levels. The first scenario outlined above provides for such an evolution with certain new initiatives placed within the WTO, although well short of the Grand Bargain proposal. The third scenario which follows adds a new regional dimension to scenario one, with potential to become the catalyst for an earlier multilateral/regional synthesis.

An Extension and Integration of Regional Free Trade

Regional free trade is already the objective for nations accounting for three-quarters of the WTO membership and 70 percent of world trade, and thus an alternative to a WTO-based Grand Bargain negotiation would be a direct linkage among the principal regional groupings to form a dominant free trade core within the trading system, which could then be expanded as circumstances permit toward global participation. Currently, the European, Western Hemisphere, and Asia-Pacific groupings are the principal candidates for such an amalgamation, but an early joint move to do so faces problems similar to those of a WTO free trade initiative. The slower pace of the APEC free trade process and the likely unwillingness of Europe and Latin America to offer free access to their markets for Asian exporters are among the major obstacles. One additional regional initiative, however, could play an immediate role for integrating all of the major groupings on an accelerated step-by-step basis, thereby greatly diminishing the threat of a drifting apart of the trading system into rival regional blocs. The initiative would be a TAFTA.

A TAFTA has received belated attention since 1994, but discussion has thus far been incomplete and disjointed, in part because North Atlantic governments have essentially backed into the subject. Both the EU and the United States were negotiating free trade agreements with much of the rest of the world, and it was becoming a more and more glaring anomaly for the NATO allies, who had formed the central axis of the GATT trading system for almost fifty years, not to be considering free trade across the Atlantic. For reasons explained more fully below, however, the United States and the EU, while establishing a New Transatlantic Agenda at a summit meeting in Madrid in December 1995, went no further than indirect reference to a TAFTA by calling for a study of possible future reduction or elimination of trade barriers.

Thus, at the official level, there is currently no serious consideration of a possible TAFTA, which is especially unfortunate because the implications of such an agreement are far-reaching, consisting of three interacting dimensions. The first dimension involves the trade and income effects of a TAFTA, both for members of the agreement and nonmember trading partners, and the second dimension is the impact on the trading system—in particular the dynamic of such an initiative on the evolving relationship between the multilateral and regional tracks. The third dimension concerns broader foreign policy considerations, which are detailed in the final section of this essay in connection with the U.S. leadership role in a greatly changed post–Cold War world order.

The economic benefits of a TAFTA between the EU/EFTA and the NAFTA countries—which is a reasonable assumption about initial membership—are difficult to assess, especially with respect to the more dynamic effects of structural changes in member economies induced by the agreement. For the nonagricultural sector, there are first the direct effects of tariff elimination: relative prices change, stimulating more trade, existing plants benefit from larger-scale production, and a slightly higher aggregate level of savings and investment is realized. Additional "dynamic" gains from trade are obtained to the extent that companies restructure their production and marketing patterns, including new investment decisions, in response to the more predictable—and competitive—transatlantic market permanently free of border restrictions. Still further gains would accrue from other elements of a TAFTA, such as inclusion of investment and competition policies, public procurement, telecommunications regulation, and industrial standards, although actions in these areas will probably move ahead, to some extent, with or without a TAFTA. The trade and income effects for the direct impact of tariff elimination are estimated to be quite small—a 2 percent increase in exports at most—but the additional dynamic effects, while almost certainly much larger, do not lend themselves to such econometric quantification, and can best be judged in more qualitative terms by surveys of corporate intent, which have not yet been done.[3]

In any event, the trade and investment effects of a TAFTA should be relatively small, on balance positive for all members, and should not provoke the kind of protectionist reaction which occurred, for example, in the United States over NAFTA, based on the fear of job losses to cheap Mexican labor. Any adverse trade impact on nonmembers should likewise be small. Half or more of nonagricultural imports would already be duty-free on an MFN basis, no tariffs would be increased through formation of a free trade agreement, as distinct from a customs union, and some tariffs might be harmonized downward during the course of negotiations.

Agriculture is often cited as a stumbling block for a TAFTA, but it need not be so, accounting for only about 5 percent of transatlantic trade. The EU is not prepared to make specific commitments for free trade at this time, but a general statement of ultimate intent, together with substantial liberalization, based on the Uruguay Round "built-in agenda," should produce an acceptable result. The Uruguay Round agreement stipulates new negotiations for liberalizing the agricultural sector by 2000, and another five-year phased reduction of MFN tariffs and export subsidies, patterned on the Uruguay Round commitments, would constitute a substantial benefit to all agricultural exporting nations. In addition, those agricultural products largely traded across the Atlantic could be subject to a phaseout of tariffs within a TAFTA, as occurred in EU free trade agreements with Central European nations. In any event, the EU needs to reform its agricultural policy further to accommodate full membership for Central Europeans, and to this end greater use could be made of income support payments to small farmers, as permitted by the WTO. An arrangement along these lines would stretch a purist interpretation of GATT Article XXIV, but this ill-defined article has experienced greater abuse for lesser cause.

The overall conclusion with respect to the substance and economic impact of a TAFTA is that they should not present major technical problems, and even the agricultural sector, while clearly the most difficult, is not nearly as daunting a challenge as it was in the 1980s. This TAFTA technical assessment, incidentally, stands in sharp contrast with the APEC free trade objective, which requires the assimilation of national economies with greatly diverse trading systems and levels of economic development.

The second dimension of a TAFTA initiative—its impact on the trading system—could be far-reaching, and would depend in large part on how the initiative is managed. There would be four largely distinct relationships to consider: Europe and the Western Hemisphere; the advanced 2010 East-Asian countries; other major trading nations; and the WTO.

1. Europe and the Western Hemisphere. This is the only relationship that can be projected with reasonable confidence. A TAFTA would almost certainly have to be open-ended through an accession clause, as is NAFTA, and with recognition that European countries linked by free trade with the EU and FTAA participants in the Western Hemisphere would be offered associate or full membership to form an extended TAFTA. The EU is already pursuing free trade initiatives with Mexico and Mercosur, the anomaly of transatlantic free trade without the United States. In fact, all of these relationships would be moving forward in parallel and likely reach a decisive stage by 2005 if not sooner. There should also be a positive attitude on all sides to attain such an extended TAFTA. Central European and South American countries should be comfortable politically and would benefit economically from free access to both the EU and NAFTA markets, while the EU and NAFTA members would no longer face high tariffs in South America and Central Europe, respectively, as they now do. In other words, the regional free trade objectives in Europe, the Western Hemisphere, and across the Atlantic should be mutually reinforcing toward accelerated implementation.

2. The Asia-Pacific 2010 APEC countries. These countries are committed to achieve free trade by 2010 within the APEC forum and will likely consist of Japan, Australia, New Zealand, and perhaps South Korea, Singapore, and Taiwan. Japan would be key, but is currently unable to decide what specific 2010 course to take, unwilling to support a preferential arrangement in the Asia-Pacific region while understanding that MFN free trade by all APEC members is unrealistic. An extended TAFTA, as described in number one above, however, even at an early stage of active consideration, would create a strong incentive for Japan to decide on its free trade course, and would permit a new and more appealing option through association with the extended TAFTA. The anticipated OECD investment agreement would provide a bridge with such a free trade agreement. Japan would have to be more forthcoming in opening its rice market, which will become easier as the dwindling number of rice farmers continues to age. As for its relationship with East Asia, Japan could follow the longstanding example of Singapore/ Hong Kong and eliminate its remaining low nonagricultural tariffs on an MFN basis within the extended TAFTA (suitably renamed), on the assumption that other APEC members would reach free trade by 2020 in their own Asian manner.

3. Other major trading nations. An extended TAFTA under number one would already include half of world trade, and linkage with the 2010 Asia-Pacific countries would raise this share considerably higher, leaving relatively few major trading nations outside the core free trade relationship. Numerous least-developed countries account for a very small share of world trade and would continue to receive preferential trade treatment, which could be enhanced. The remaining major countries would be in East and South Asia—ASEAN, China, India/Pakistan—and Russia/Ukraine, and their relationships with the core free trade grouping would vary considerably. ASEAN countries and China are committed to free trade within the Asia-Pacific region by 2020. India and Pakistan, in contrast, remain primarily engaged within the WTO multilateral trading system, except for consideration of a South Asia regional trade arrangement, while Russia and Ukraine would likely find an early TAFTA free trade association attractive. Initial reactions from these trading partners would likely be questioning or critical, and a principal objective of the leaders of the TAFTA-extended

grouping vis-à-vis these other countries would be to demonstrate that the free trade relationship is not exclusionary and is
based on reducing rather than raising trade barriers.[4] The
longer-term objective would be to integrate the remaining countries within the core grouping while recognizing that they need
more time and should proceed at their own pace.

4. The WTO. The final step for a multilateral/regional synthesis within this scenario would involve integrating the core
free trade agreement with the WTO. A TAFTA extended to European and Western Hemisphere countries would already include
the majority of WTO members and global trade, and further
extension to the APEC 2010 countries would add much of the
remainder. Integrating this arrangement within the WTO would
thus require more than simply depositing documents in
Geneva, and some significant changes in the current WTO structure would be required. A name change to the World Trade and
Investment Organization (WTIO) will in any event be likely over
the next several years. Conditional MFN between members of
the free trade grouping and others, at least for some parts of the
core agreement, would likely be necessary. Voting procedures
would also have to be amended as they applied to implementation of parts of the core free trade agreement. The net result,
however, should be a greatly enhanced multilateral trading system within which the multilateral/regional synthesis would be
definitively realized, and procedures established to broaden the
inner free trade grouping as other nations become willing and
able to participate. Moreover, the whole process of assimilation
could be assisted by multilateral actions emanating from the
WTO work program, perhaps in the context of a new round of
multilateral negotiations.

This scenario of the consequences of a TAFTA initiative on
the overall trading system demonstrates the powerful dynamic
that would be unleashed by such an initiative and which could
set the most favorable course toward achieving a relatively early
multilateral/regional synthesis. The critical role of political leadership and management, however, cannot be overemphasized.
Relationships between TAFTA leaders and those of other major
trading nations—Japan, China, ASEAN, India, Russia, and
Brazil—will be critical to the outcome, and need to be developed
carefully so as to minimize conflict and ensure a mutually beneficial outcome. These relationships, moreover, go beyond trade
or even the broadened trade/investment/technology economic
relationship under discussion here. A wide range of foreign
policy interests will be influenced by trade strategies pursued in

the period ahead, under any of the foregoing scenarios, and particularly with respect to a decision regarding a TAFTA. For many observers, indeed, the foreign policy dimension of a TAFTA initiative is paramount.

The Foreign Policy and Leadership Dimension

Economic globalization, including the deepening integration of national economic policies, has far-reaching foreign policy consequences, especially in the post–Cold War circumstances in which longstanding East-West security alliances have lost most of their raison d'etre. Foreign policy interests need to be reordered with greater emphasis on economic relationships, but not to the exclusion of reformulated national security interests and broader geopolitical considerations. The difficulties in such a reordering are evident in the subject addressed here, the evolving multilateral/regional structure of the world trading system. In particular, the choice between the current course in scenario one and the projected scenario three featuring a TAFTA initiative can only be judged fully by taking account of the broader foreign policy implications, which are, in fact, of greater consequence than the economic effects for a trading system which in any event is working its way in the direction of more and more open trade.

A major foreign policy question involved is whether the Atlantic Alliance, post–Cold War, is drifting apart in politico-economic terms into what could become rival regional blocs and, if so, how the choice of trade strategy over the next several years could affect the outcome. European nations are focused on historic opportunities to the East and on troubled neighbors in the Mediterranean Basin while the declining U.S. troop presence in Europe makes America an increasingly distant ally. The United States, in parallel, is shifting its geographic priorities to the Western Hemisphere and across the Pacific, largely in pursuit of commercial interests. In each case, a central policy objective is a regional free trade arrangement with inevitable exclusionary consequences across the Atlantic. Trade and investment continue to flourish between Europe and North America, but multinational companies tend to adjust to whatever policy frameworks are encountered, and the current course may not be enough to maintain the longstanding transatlantic political/security/economic cohesion. As one European leader concluded: "The glue, which kept us together for so long, has lost its strength."[5]

There is no question that a TAFTA would produce a new cohesive construct for the industrialized democracies of Europe and North America to confront the emerging post–Cold War challenges to global stability and security. The threat of a drifting apart into rival geopolitical groupings would be greatly reduced if not eliminated. As noted earlier, future extension of the European free trade grouping to Russia and other former Soviet republics would not create the foreign policy difficulties for the United States and the EU with a TAFTA in place as they would without one. Within Europe, the objective of political integration and economic union should not be threatened by a phasing-out across the Atlantic of the remaining Common External Tariff, already quite low and no longer the major cohesive element it once was for the European Community.

The most complex foreign policy implications for a TAFTA would be with respect to Asia, and a careful assessment of how this relationship would be managed should be an important part of an overall TAFTA evaluation. The tentative judgement here is that it could be managed to positive effect. Japan and South Korea, as industrialized democracies, should continue to be drawn more closely together with Europe and North America through various political and economic forums, including the WTO and the OECD. A TAFTA could work to accelerate this process. ASEAN members, India, and other Asia nations all have to be given assurances that a faster track to free trade elsewhere is not at their expense, which could be done as explained in note 4 of this essay. The Chinese relationship would clearly require the most careful attention, but a trade strategy as contained in scenario three, with the United States in a central position within a more cohesive grouping of industrialized democracies in Europe and the Western Hemisphere, could provide a stronger basis, compared with the current course, for the undoubtedly difficult and relatively long-term objective of positive Chinese participation in the global political and economic systems.

Any successful trade strategy at this juncture will require strong and sustained political leadership, and the TAFTA-oriented scenario three particularly so. Forward-looking U.S. leadership, moreover, will remain essential for at least the five-to ten-year time horizon addressed here, even though trade policy leadership is broadening compared with the earlier predominant U.S. role. The EU, in the 1990s, has displayed more pronounced leadership on trade issues, but its decision-making procedures are cumbersomely slow and its preoccupation with regional objectives continues, while Japan is reluctant to take on a global leadership role commensurate with its economic power. Newly industrialized nations are more actively engaged than a decade ago, but they still tend to be reactive to initiatives taken by the more advanced industrialized countries.

The traditional inspired U.S. leadership, however, has been conspicuously lacking in recent years, and especially during 1995–97. The earlier Uruguay Round and NAFTA initiatives were concluded and regional free trade objectives in the Western Hemisphere and the Asia-Pacific region agreed to in principle by 1994, but little follow-on has taken place since then. The U.S. response to interest by others in a TAFTA since 1994 is especially revealing. Canadian Prime Minister Jean Chrétien and various European leaders called for a serious look at a TAFTA in view of the proliferation of regional free trade initiatives elsewhere. The U.S. response was initially one of disinterest, then grudging agreement to an EU proposal in May 1995 to give TAFTA "the serious study it deserves," and then dilution of the study pro-posal by the time of the December U.S.-EU summit in Madrid, whereby indirect reference to examine ways of "further reducing or eliminating tariff and non-tariff barriers" would limit exami-nation of a possible TAFTA to its narrow technical aspects.

This hiatus in U.S. trade policy leadership is due, in part, to domestic politics and the decision of leaders in both major par-ties to downplay support for a liberal trade policy in the run-up to the 1996 elections. It also reflects a tendency, post–Cold War, to view U.S. global interests in more narrowly defined commer-cial terms, and thus to avoid global strategizing within which trade policy plays a major but not the only role. And finally, the hiatus reflects an intellectual vacuum within the U.S. govern-ment, a general lack of interest or capacity to give serious consideration to the broader questions of trade strategy, while "the vision thing" remains in bipartisan disrepute.

It was not always this way, of course. The leaders in the United States and Europe who created the Bretton Woods sys-tem, including the GATT, in the wake of the Great Depression and the devastation of World War II, combined vision with forceful action. So, too, did the postwar leaders who launched the Marshall Plan, NATO, and the Common Market, to achieve both a democratic reconciliation between France and Germany after three wars in three successive generations and a political-security bulwark against the external Soviet threat. By compari-son, the circumstances of the post–Cold War world, while far from trouble-free, present extraordinary positive opportunities. The industrialized democracies are broadening in geographic scope and influence. The rapid growth of international trade and investment constitutes a massive positive sum game from which all nations should benefit. The leadership challenge today is to build on a dynamic growing concern rather than reconstruction of a crippled and threatened enterprise.

The leadership focus for trade strategy, beginning in 1997, is not clear. For governments, the biannual WTO ministerial meetings are very large and unwieldy gatherings. The annual G-7 economic summit meetings of the major industrialized nations are dominated by finance ministers with principal interests in macroeconomic policy and international financial markets rather than trade strategy. The informal, "Quad" relationship of trade ministers from the United States, the EU, Japan, and Canada comes closest to a high-level trade strategy grouping, at least among the industrialized countries, but trade ministers tend to be hard bargainers over immediate interests rather than longer-term strategizers.

In any event, discussion of trade strategy at this important juncture should be more broadly based than official intergovernmental deliberations. Legislators, private sector leaders, and others outside of government need to become engaged. An assessment of the full consequences of a TAFTA, for example, would benefit from a U.S.-European parliamentary dialogue and consideration by private sector leaders within the recently established Transatlantic Business Dialogue. An Eminent Persons Group, which played a catalytic role in formulating the Asia-Pacific free trade objective, should also be formed to evaluate a TAFTA initiative, but this EPG should be of different composition, consisting principally of former statesmen and other distinguished public and private sector leaders rather than of economists/technocrats as was the case for APEC, since the questions to be addressed with respect to a TAFTA initiative are of broader political and economic scope.

The challenge of getting from here to free trade is more than a phrase. It is an operational objective for going forward at both the multilateral and regional levels. How the objective is pursued, including the quest for a synthesis between the multilateral and regional tracks, requires urgent consideration and probably bold action. It is also too important a task to be left to government leaders alone.

Notes

Essay 1

1. English-speaking economists don't even agree on the proper spelling of the term. In London, one reads of globalisation. The difference in spelling spills over to international organizations. The OECD, with predominant European participation and roots, uses globalisation, while the WTO, reflecting the activist U.S. role over the decades in its GATT predecessor, writes of globalization.

2. Such episodic reports come preponderantly from critics of a liberal trade policy who decry the negative impact of globalization. In the political arena, protectionist demagogues Ross Perot and Pat Buchanan are striking examples. In the media, the lengthy series of articles in the Philadelphia Inquirer, by Pulitzer Prize–winning journalists Donald Barlett and James Steele constitutes an extraordinary example of the use of personal interviews and highly misleading summary statements to show how economic globalization produces substantial adverse results for the United States. The series, entitled "America: Who Stole the Dream?," ran from 8 September to 22 September 1996.

3. An alternate basis for assessing economic globalization would be the degree of movement toward a unified market, wherein prices would be unified except for differences in transportation costs. The international banking sector, for example, may be approaching such unification now (and with negligible transportation costs). The EC-92 market unification program was also based on such an objective. For the foreseeable future, however, the global economy has many impediments to full market unification, including the relative immobility of labor, and policy interest is concentrated on the implications of the cross-border economic activities that make up the economic globalization definition presented in the text.

4. A summary of the nineteenth-century commentary is contained in Malcolm Waters, *Globalization* (London: Routledge, 1995), chap. 1. The Marx quote is on p. 6.

5. Paul Krugman, *Peddling Prosperity: Economic Sense and Nonsense in the Age of Dimension Expectations* (New York: W. W. Norton and Co., 1994), 258. A critique of the Krugman trade assessment is contained in Ernest H. Preeg, "Krugmanian Competitiveness: A Dangerous Obfuscation," *The Washington Quarterly*, Autumn 1994, 111–22.

6. WTO, *International Trade: Trends and Statistics* (Geneva: 1995), 17. The quote is drawn from the section entitled "The Pace of Global Integration," 15–22.

7. OECD Development Centre, Policy brief no. 11 (Paris: 1996). Oman's analysis is elaborated in his earlier study, *Globalisation and Regionalisation: The Challenge for Developing Countries*, also published by the OECD Development Centre, 1994.

8. The "three waves" of economic globalization presented here are distinct from the more familiar "three waves" in the 1980 Alvin and Heidi Toffler book, *The Third Wave*, consisting of the agricultural, industrial, and information revolutions, although there is a convergence of the two third waves. Unfortunately, the Toffler book is an example of the "forest" type analysis—sweeping commentary about global change, in futuristic terms, with few specific conclusions.

9. WTO, *International Trade*, 16.

10. Ibid., 17–18

11. WTO, "Trade and Foreign Direct Investment" (Geneva: 9 October 1996), 21.

12. The figures for FDI in this and the two succeeding paragraphs are from UNCTAD, *World Investment Report*, 1996.

13. Oman, *Globalisation and Regionalisation*, 1996, 20–26. Another statement along these lines is contained in the chapter, "Organizing for Innovation: The Multinational Enterprise in the Twenty-first Century," by Peter J. Buckley and Mark Casson, in Buckley and Casson, eds., *Multinational Enterprises in the World Economy: Essays in Honor of John Dunning* (Aldershot: Edward Elgar Publishing Company, 1992). Their central theme is, "Existing management practices—even in quite sophisticated MNEs—seem to be geared too little to the management of innovation and too much to the management of routine" (212).

14. UNCTAD, *World Investment Report* (Geneva: 1996), 89.

15. The figures for FDI in this paragraph are from the World Bank, *World Debt Tables: External Finance for Developing Countries*, volume 1 (1996), 3. Note that the figure for FDI to developing countries, $90 billion, differs from the $100 billion in the UNCTAD *World Investment Report*, cited in note 12 above. The difference is due to country coverage. The World Bank excludes, most significantly, Bermuda, Hong Kong, Singapore, and Taiwan, which are included in the UNCTAD figures.

16. The two stages, in practice, are not that distinct. Foreign students work in the United States to help pay their way though college, thus becoming partly immigrant labor and partly foreign purchaser of U.S. services. The subsidized portion of foreign student education, moreover, should be considered a form of economic aid, and in fact is probably the most cost-effective of all U.S. economic aid programs in terms of development impact.

17. A useful summary of recent theoretical work on the relationship between FDI and trade is contained in UNCTAD, *World Investment Report*, 123–25.

18. I wish to express special thanks to Gary Hufbauer for the idea of presenting summary indicators, as in table 3, for a "strong discontinuity story," although the substantive assessment remains the sole responsibility of the author.

19. See GATT, *The Results of the Uruguay Round of Multilateral Trade Negotiations* (Geneva: November 1994).

20. An example of such precisely wrong reporting is contained in Lester C. Thurow, *The Future of Capitalism: How Today's Economic Forces Shape Tomorrow's World* (New York: William Morrow and Company, 1996), 132: "The World Bank, the IMF, and the GATT predict that what was agreed upon in Geneva will raise the world GDP by $140 to $274 billion by 2002. . . . Even the maximum gain . . . means there will be a little less than a one percent increase in world GDP." The static gains figures are from "GATT Deal May Enrich World by $270 Billion," *Financial Times*, 10 November 1993, which makes no allowances for the dynamic gains.

21. For a survey of recent literature, see *The Dynamic Effects of Trade Liberalization: A Survey*, United States International Trade Commission (USITC) publication 2608 (Washington, D.C., February 1993). In a June 1994 publication, *Potential Impact on the U.S. Economy and Industries of the GATT Uruguay Round Agreements*, the USITC concludes, "The long-run dynamic effects of trade liberalization may be two to three times the static estimates" (vol. 1, I-13).

22. The December 1996 report of the five economist Commission, led by Michael Boskin, estimated an annual overstatement of inflation of 1.1 percent, based on a range of 0.8 to 1.6 percent. Since the report was related to budget reforms that would reduce the growth in entitlements and tax benefits, one member of the Commission explained, "we've taken every opportunity to err on the conservative side" ("Economic Scene; The Hard Part: Fixing the Errant Price Index," *New York Times*, 5 December 1996). Unfortunately, subsequent debate polarized between those who would gain and those who would lose from the budget effects, although Boskin did make the broader point about the implications for the economy as a whole: "Real median family income (from 1973 to 1995) grew 36 percent, not the puny four percent in the official statistics" ("Prisoners of Faulty Statistics," *Wall Street Journal*, 5 December 1996*)*. Further support for a higher U.S. income growth experience than reflected in official statistics derives from sharply higher levels of consumption, including restaurant meals, vacation trips, consumer electronics, college tuition payments, and health care services. Information along these lines is provided at various points in Robert J. Samuelson, *The Good Life and Its Discontents* (New York: Times Books, 1995).

23. The impact of the first three years of NAFTA on U.S. jobs is estimated as a loss of 28,000 jobs to imports offset by a gain of 31,000 in export-related jobs. An additional 33,000 jobs losses are attributed to plant relocations in Mexico. See "NAFTA's Impact on Employment is Slight, Study Says," *New York Times*, 19 December 1996, related to a study by a UCLA research team.

24. William R. Cline, *Trade and Wage Inequality* (Washington, D.C.: Institute for International Economics, forthcoming). The quote is from a draft of November 1996.

25. This subject is treated in greater detail in an unpublished essay by the author entitled, "The Trillion Dollar Foreign Debt, a Strong Dollar, and the International Exchange Rate System."

26. Although U.S. dependency on imported oil is high and likely to go higher, the threat of a major cutback of foreign oil supplies and the degree of ensuing adverse impact on the U.S. economy may be less than they were in the 1970s for a number of reasons.

27. This point is elaborated in Ernest H. Preeg, *Traders in a Brave New World: The Uruguay Round and the Future of the International Trading System* (Chicago: University of Chicago Press, 1995), 236: "The utopian New Soviet Man never materialized, but the New High-tech Economic Person is already among us and exercising a growing influence. These new economic persons have a common educational grounding across national borders based on scientific inquiry and the rule of reason. They have an optimistic disposition, working within the enormous positive sum game environment of new technology development and application, and are negatively disposed to economic nationalism that holds back technological change. At the international level, they communicate freely with each other despite widely differing cultural background and provide the expertise and leadership for the economic globalization under way. They are engineers, scientists, economists, business-school graduates, and technicians nurtured on computers and jointly able to create amazing new technology-intensive enterprises oriented toward international trade and investment. They are the traders in a brave new economic world, and their eighteenth-century forefathers would be very proud of them."

Essay 2

1. See Anne O. Krueger, *American Trade Policy: A Tragedy in the Making* (Washington D.C.: AEI Press, 1995), 6–7.

2. A fuller discussion of the economic benefits and political considerations for free trade in the automotive sector is contained in Ernest H. Preeg, "Free Trade in Automobiles," *The Journal of Commerce*, 15 May 1997.

3. Speaker Gingrich proposed a TAFTA as well as a free trade agreement with Japan in his first full-length speech on foreign policy at a CSIS meeting on 18 July 1995; Henry Kissinger called for a TAFTA in an op-ed piece in the *Washington Post*, 12 May 1995.

4. For example, in the Uruguay Round agreement, developing countries reduced nonagricultural tariffs by 20 percent (compared with 40 percent for industrialized countries), had similar lower obligations for agricultural tariffs, and did not have to phase out quotas in the textiles and apparel sector. They likewise undertook a narrower range of market access commitments for trade in services, received a longer transition period for

implementation for intellectual proper rights and other obligations, and did not join the government procurement agreement.

5. The EU subscribes to a policy of regional subsidies favoring its lower-income members, but this differential treatment is apart from the fully reciprocal basis of the trade policy relationship.

6. Antidumping procedures can more easily be eliminated once free trade is established because exports sold at unfairly low prices can be "dumped back" in the exporting country market. The link to competition policy, among other things, is to make sure such dumping back can take place.

7. For example, two leading free trade economists, Krueger again and Jagdish Bhagwati, have accentuated the negative about regional free trade agreements, with Bhagwati concluding that such a policy is a mistake. See their *The Dangerous Drift to Preferential Trade Agreements* (Washington, D.C.: AEI Press, 1995).

Essay 3

1. Ellen L. Frost, *Transatlantic Trade: a Strategic Agenda*, (Washington, D.C.: Institute for International Economics, 1997). This study also contains a comprehensive bibliography of recent work on the subject.

2. Richard Baldwin and Joseph Francois, "Transatlantic Free Trade: A Quantitative Assessment," unpublished, May 1996 (final version). The authors are affiliated with the Centre for Economic Policy Research, Graduate Institute for International Studies, Geneva, and also advise the WTO, although the views expressed in this paper "are strictly those of the authors."

3. "The New Transatlantic Agenda," Madrid, Spain, 3 December 1995, signed by President Bill Clinton, Prime Minister Felipe Gonzalez of Spain, and European Commission President Jacques Santer.

4. Such varying views can be found in Bruce Stokes, ed., *Open for Business: Creating a Transatlantic Marketplace*, (New York: Council on Foreign Relations, 1996).

5. A CSIS group report, chaired by Senator Lugar, Congressman Hamilton, and Zbigniew Brzezinski, recommends that the United States, "lay the groundwork for a transatlantic free trade initiative that builds on the Clinton administration's transatlantic agenda." See *Foreign Policy into the 21st Century: The U.S. Leadership Challenge* (Washington, D.C.: CSIS, 1996), 24.

Essay 4

1. Most of the information presented in this section was obtained during 1996–97 through the OAS via website (http://www.sice.oas.org), including the working group reports and statements made at the March 1996 ministerial meeting at Cartagena, Colombia, and the May 1997 ministerial meeting in Belo Horizonte, Brazil. A summary of the FTAA preparations up

to the June 1995 ministerial meeting in Denver, Colorado, is contained in OAS, *Interim Report of the OAS Special Committee on Trade to the Western Hemisphere Trade Ministerial* (Washington, D.C.: 1995). A supporting analysis of the changing structure of trade in the hemisphere is provided in *Economic Integration in the Americas: 1995 Year-End Report,* Inter-American Development Bank, (Washington, D.C.: February 1996).

2. During NAFTA negotiations and now within preliminary FTAA discussions, the objective of tariff harmonization within a sector has been raised as a means to avoid the need for a rules of origin test, but the same logic would carry over for the broader concept of only high tariff country application of rules of origin tests.

3. U.S. pressures for higher domestic content by Japanese auto transplants in the United States, incidentally, were contradictory to the simultaneous U.S. objective in the Uruguay Round to eliminate such performance requirements for foreign investors within the trade-related investment measures negotiations.

4. The United States also continues a foreign direct investment screening process related to national security which is unlikely to be applied against Canadian or Mexican nationals.

5. Technical support staff for such reports is supplied mainly by the OAS and to a lesser extent by the Inter-American Development Bank and the UN Economic Commission for Latin America and the Caribbean. Members of the OAS Trade Unit were most helpful in providing background information and commenting on earlier versions of this essay.

6. SPS stands for sanitary and phytosanitary, in keeping with Uruguay Round terminology, while the FTAA working group uses SFM for sanitary and phytosanitary measures. There is also a variation in spelling in the working group report—both phyto and phitosanitary are used.

7. "Americas Trade" (formerly "Inside NAFTA"), 29 May 1997.

8. The Clinton Administration three-year report of 11 July 1997, focusing on the increase in higher paying export-related jobs, concluded that NAFTA has had a "modest positive effect" on the U.S. economy. In a broader assessment, *NAFTA at Three: A Progress Report* (Washington D.C.: CSIS, 1997), Sidney Weintraub stresses the benefits from growth in U.S.-Mexican trade in both directions, as well as broader improvements in the bilateral relationship: "The liaisons between Americans and Mexicans are growing in ways that never existed before. . . . NAFTA is enveloping the two countries in more cooperative relations than existed earlier."

Essay 5

1. The assessment of the Canberra meeting is taken from Ernest H. Preeg, "Rationale, Objectives and Modalities," contained in Richard L. Grant, et al., *Asia Pacific Economic Cooperation: The Challenge Ahead* (Washington, D.C.: CSIS, 1990), 13–47.

2. See Ernest H. Preeg, "Next, a Free-Trade Pact with Japan?" *Wall Street Journal,* 12 August 1988.

3. Jeffrey J. Schott, ed., *Free Trade Areas and U.S. Trade Policy* (Washington, D.C.: Institute for International Economics, 1989).

4. An in-depth examination of U.S. trade policy decision-making during 1994 would be well worth a Ph.D. dissertation. The Clinton administration, in the author's assessment, belatedly and somewhat reluctantly backed into regional free trade commitments in the Asia-Pacific region and the Western Hemisphere (at the Miami summit meeting) in November-December 1994, with considerable last minute urging from the private sector. The principal trade policy focus for the administration during most of the year had been Congressional approval of the Uruguay Round agreement, which dragged out until November, and the overriding, highly politicized debate in Washington concerned the administration's ill-fated health care proposal leading to the Republican electoral victory in the Congress. The trade strategy question is whether the definitive move of the United States to seek broad-based regional free trade with East Asia and within the Americas was a consciously developed multilateral/regional design or an outcome backed into during the largely ad hoc and politically turbulent course of events.

5. Open regionalism could include unilateral liberalization, liberalization internally on an MFN basis, extension of regional liberalization to nonmembers on a mutually reciprocal basis, and unilateral extension of APEC liberalization to nonmembers on a conditional or unconditional basis. See APEC, *Achieving the APEC Vision: Free and Open Trade in the Asia-Pacific* (Singapore: 1994), 30.

6. The Philippine objective, announced earlier, formed the basis of the Philippine individual action plan at Subic Bay.

7. Ippei Yamazawa, "APEC's New Development and Its Implications for Non-Member Developing Countries," *Developing Economics,* June 1996, 133.

8. Russia also wanted to participate in the first ASEM, as the only country that is both European and Asian, but no invitation was forthcoming.

Essay 6

1. From a speech given in Ottawa on 28 May 1996.

2. C. Fred Bergsten, "Globalizing Free Trade," *Foreign Affairs,* May/June 1996, 105–20.

3. The up to 2 percent estimate is taken from Richard Baldwin and Joseph Francois, "Transatlantic Free Trade: A Quantitative Assessment," May 1996 (unpublished), and described in greater detail in essay 3. The survey of corporate intent could be undertaken by the private sector Transatlantic Business Dialogue established in 1995.

4. An anticipated negative reaction from Asians is the most frequent argument made against a TAFTA, argued most strenuously by proponents of APEC, and a full consideration of their concern is in order. A starting point for explaining a TAFTA in positive terms to Asian trading partners would be: A TAFTA would do nothing more than achieve the free trade objective already engaged across the Pacific between North America and East Asia, as well as in other regions. Indeed, in the process underway toward global free trade, the North Atlantic nations should be among the first rather than the last to eliminate border restrictions to trade on a regional basis since they are the most mature and open industrialized economies, with import barriers already much lower than in other regions, including zero on an MFM basis for half of nonagricultural imports. Moreover, no trade barriers would be raised to Asian exporters in the formation of a TAFTA.

5. The quote is attributed to Belgian Prime Minister Jean-Luc Dehaene in Bruce Stokes, ed., *Open for Business: Creating a Transatlantic Marketplace* (New York: Council on Foreign Relations, 1996), 2.

Credits

Earlier versions of essays 2–6, used here with permission, appear in the following publications:

Essay 2: "The Post–Uruguay Round Free Trade Debate," *The Washington Quarterly* 19, no. 1 (winter 1996): 223–38. © 1995 by The Center for Strategic and International Studies and the Massachusetts Institute of Technology.

Essay 3: "The Policy Forum: Transatlantic Free Trade," *The Washington Quarterly* 19, no. 2 (spring 1996): 105–33. © 1996 by The Center for Strategic and International Studies and the Massachusetts Institute of Technology.

Essay 4: "Rival or Mutually Reinforcing Regulatory Regimes in World Trade? The Case of NAFTA and FTAA," chap. 5 in *Towards Rival Regionalism? US and EU Regional Regulatory Regime Building,* ed. Jens van Scherpenberg and Elke Thiel (Baden-Baden: Nomos Verlag, 1998). © 1998 by Stiftung Wissenschaft und Politik.

Essay 5: "APEC, ASEM, and the New Transatlantic Agenda (TAFTA?): An Unequal Interacting Triad," in *The Future of APEC,* ed. Jacques Pelkmans and Hiroko Shinkai (Brussels: European Institute for South and South-east Asia, 1998).

Essay 6: "From Here to Free Trade: The Quest for a Multilateral/ Regional Synthesis," in *Trade Strategy for a New Era: Ensuring U.S. Leadership in a Global Economy,* ed. Geza Feketekuty with Bruce Stokes (New York: The Council on Foreign Relations in association with the Monterey Institute of International Studies, 1997).

Index